The Bible On
The Preaching Of The Word

The Bible

on

The Preaching

of The Word

by J. KAHMANN, CSSR

Translated by T. J. HOLMES

ST. NORBERT ABBEY PRESS
De Pere, Wisconsin
U. S. A.
1965

Biblical quotations are from the Revised Standard Version of the Bible, copyrighted 1946 and 1952 by the Division of Christian Education, National Council of Churches, and used by permission.

Nihil obstat:
>Samuel D. Jadin, O. Praem.
>Censor deputatus

Imprimatur:
>†Stanislaus V. Bona, D.D.
>Bishop of Green Bay
>November 15, 1965

>The *Nihil obstat* and *Imprimatur* are a declaration that a book or pamphlet is considered free from doctrinal or moral error. It is not implied that those who have granted the *Nihil obstat* and *Imprimatur* agree with the contents, opinions or statements expressed.

Originally published as
De Bijbel over de prediking van het Woord
Roermond and Maaseik, J. J. Romen & Zonen, 1961

Library of Congress catalogue card number: 65 - 29090

Printed in the United States of America
ST. NORBERT ABBEY PRESS
De Pere, Wisconsin

CONTENTS

FOREWORD

"Proclaim the word; deliver it, welcome or not." This command given by Paul to Timothy is a command to the Church for all time.

The Catholic people of our time are showing renewed interest in the sermon. Sometimes this interest shows itself in a criticism of "preaching"; yet its deepest origins lie in an understanding — or at least an unconscious appreciation — of what preaching means to the Church, and of what Christ intended it to be.

There is a search going on for new forms and methods in this area. This search must be based on a clear consideration of the vital importance of preaching for Christ's work of salvation and upon an understanding of what preaching really is.

This little book explains what the New Testament has to say about preaching; it hopes to be of some use to priests and laymen in their considerations.

THE FACT OF PREACHING

"In many and various ways God spoke of old to our fathers by the prophets; but in these last days he has spoken to us by a Son" (Hebr. 1, 1-2). This text sees God as speaking through those whom he has sent — which is what we mean by **preaching** — as the heart of the Old and New Testament. When this was written, the preaching of the New Testament had reached the boundaries of the then known world. Paul tells us this toward the end of his apostolic career, when he says of the preachers: "Their voice has gone out to all the earth, and their words to the ends of the world" (Rom. 10, 18). Mark's gospel closes with this testimony: "They (the apostles) went forth and preached everywhere" (Mk. 16, 20).

The preaching of the word set out on its way from Jerusalem. In the Acts of the Apostles we read regularly about its progress: "And the word of God increased" (Acts 6, 7). "But the word of God grew and multiplied" (Acts 12, 24). "And the word of the Lord spread throughout all of the region" (Acts 8, 49). In Ephesus Paul preached for two years, "so that all the residents of Asia heard the word of the Lord, both Jews and Greeks" (Acts 19, 10). "So the word of the Lord grew and prevailed mightily" (Acts 19, 20). Imprisoned in Rome, Paul reviews the harvest of the preaching. He writes to the church of Colossa about "the word of the truth, the gospel which has come to you, as indeed in the whole world it is bearing fruit and growing" (Col. 1, 6).

The word of the divine messengers is vital for the New Testament. The Book of Revelation of St. John the apostle, the last book of the Bible, declares its wish to remain in the Church as a prophetic word — with a view to the end of time: "Blessed is he who reads aloud the words of the prophecy, and blessed are those who hear, and who keep what is written therein" (Rev. 1, 3). "And he (Jesus) said to me: 'Do not seal up the words of the prophecy of this book, for the time is near'" (Rev. 22, 10).

The preaching of the New Testament is not only remarkable for its expansive power. It is something which radically changes the lives of those touched by it; it makes new persons of them. The Christian community is what it is through the preaching of the word: "You have been born anew, not of perishable seed but of imperishable, through the living and abiding word of God . . . That word is the good news (gospel) which was preached to you" (1 Pet. 1, 23-25).

The preaching of the New Testament is the continuation of God's speaking "to our fathers by the prophets." The Old Testament is also permeated with preaching. The line of preachers — here the prophets — is headed by Moses. The earliest tradition of Israel shows him at Mt. Sinai as the privileged, but also the lonely; he stands between God and his people, to temper the Lord's terrible words into human terms: "Now when all the people perceived the thunderings and the lightnings and the sound of the trumpet and the mountain smoking, they were afraid and trembled; and they stood afar off, and said to Moses: 'You speak to us, and we will hear; but let not God speak to us, lest we die'" (Ex. 20, 18-19). Prophets appear in all subsequent periods. At certain times the prophetic word was scarce, and this was felt painfully in Israel. This at any rate seems to be the undertone of a message from the time of Samuel: "The word of the Lord was rare in those days; there was no frequent vision" (1 Sam. 3, 1). A similar nostalgia speaks from the first book of Maccabees, which places us shortly before the time of Christ: "So there broke out a violent persecution in Israel, such as there had not been since the times that a prophet had last been seen" (1 Macc. 9, 27).

The centuries between Samuel and the Macabees are charged with the word of the prophets. The Old Testament books are witness to this, although much of the preaching by the prophets was never written down. The prophetic word becomes a loud calling to Israel. God instructs those whom he sends: "Go and proclaim in the hearing of Jerusalem . . ." (Jer. 2, 2). "Cry aloud, spare not, lift up your voice like a trumpet" (Is. 58, 1). The ceaselessness and urgency of the prophetic preaching is particularly well stated by Jeremiah. God speaks: "From the day that your fathers came out of the land of Egypt to this day, I have persistently sent all my servants the prophets to them, day after day; yet they did not listen to me" (Jer. 7, 25-26). Jeremiah says of himself: "For twenty-three years, from the thirteenth year of Josiah the son of Amon, king of Juda, to this day the word of the Lord has come to me, and I have spoken to you from the early morning into the late evening, but you have not listened" (Jer. 25, 3). The phrase "early morning into the late evening" in this and in similar texts is a literal rendering of the Hebrew. It means, more or less, "persisting throughout the entire daytime." God leaves Israel no respite; he seems, as it were, not to rest himself nor let his prophet rest; the preaching may not stop.

The preaching of the word is of such essential importance for the relationship between God and his people that it **must** be spoken, even if Israel does not listen. This is the command given to Ezekiel: "I send you to them; and you shall say to them: 'Thus says the Lord God.' And whether they hear or refuse to hear (for they are an intractable people) they will know that there has been a prophet among them" (Ezek. 2, 4-5). In a vision the prophet is given a scroll to eat, which is written upon inside and out. He takes the fullness of God's word to himself, to be able to preach ceaselessly without tiring.

In this way the preaching by the divine messen-

gers has become one with the history of God's people
in Old and New Testament. It would seem to be an
intrinsic necessity of this history. It can be continually felt as the presence of God among his people.
This it can be, because it comes out of the pro-
foundity of God; it is **the word of God.** This is the
highest claim which the prophets make for their
preaching: "Thus says the Lord God. . . ." — the
oracle of the Lord.

The two following chapters are intended to place
— in quite a general way — the concept of preaching
against the background of God's word in Old and
New Testament.

them a prophet like you from among their brethren; and I will put my words in his mouth, and he shall speak to them all that I shall command him' " (Deut. 18, 15-18). The prophet (the word is used here in the collective sense) is God's interpreter, or God's "mouth" as we sometimes find, and as such he continues to carry out Moses' mission. His vocation is therefore closely connected with that which is the very basis of Israel's existence as God's people — the **Covenant.** He interprets the will and the plans of the God of the Covenant. It was already pointed out in the previous chapter that Israel's life for centuries bears the stamp of God's word through the mouths of the prophets. God's redeeming presence among his people becomes in fact synonymous with that word: "Behold the days are coming, says the Lord God, when I will send a famine on the land; not a famine of bread, nor a thirst for water, but of hearing the words of the Lord" (Amos 8, 11).

To the Semitic mind the word is a **dynamic** thing, charged with power. Blessing and cursing bring what they say into effect. This applies in the highest degree to God's word: it is creative, redeeming, enlivening, or — in certain circumstances — punishing and destroying. The creative nature of God's word lends support to the presentation in Genesis 1 of the creation of heaven and earth. The book of Wisdom gives a clear presentation of the intervention of God's word at one of the turning-points in Israel's history — the liberation from Egypt: "Whilst all was surrounded in stillness, and the night was half-accomplished, your all-powerful word sprang down — as a fierce warrior — from your king's throne in heaven into this decayed land — and it carried your irrevocable command as a sharpened dagger. There it stood, and everywhere it spread death — and as it strode over the earth it was as high as the heavens" (Wisd. 18, 14-16). In this text — which belongs to one of the last books of the Old Testament — we find the word of God portrayed very much as a **person.** The Old Testament at this point comes very close to the New Testament, where the ideal Witness of God — Jesus Christ — is described by John the evangelist as "the Word."

The dynamic character of God's word also applies fully to the **prophetic** word. This is shown by a passage in the vocation-vision of Jeremiah: "Then the Lord put forth his hand and touched my mouth; and the Lord said to me: 'Behold, I have put my words in your mouth. See, I have set you this day over nations and kingdoms, to pluck up and to break down, to destroy and to overthrow, to build and to plant'" (Jer. 1, 9-10). All this is to be the effect of the word of a **prophet.** The prophetic word is "like fire . . . and like a hammer which breaks the rock in pieces" (Jer. 23, 29). God hurls his word at sinful Israel as a stone which crushes (Is. 9, 7). But he also makes it the executor of his plan of salvation: "For as the rain and the snow come down from heaven, and return not thither but water the earth, making it bring forth and sprout, giving seed to the sower and bread to the eater, so shall my word be that goes forth from my mouth; it shall not return to me empty, but it shall accomplish that which I purpose, and prosper in the thing for which I sent it" (Is. 55, 10-11). Here once again is meant the word of the prophet, through whom God informs his people of the liberation from exile. Once it is spoken it sets history in motion — its effect can no longer be blocked.

We are dealing here with a concept of the word which differs greatly from the purely logical aspect, the aspect of the word as expression of a thought. In the biblical world the word is backed by the will and the entire person. Where God is concerned the word is like a spark, with which his power and goodness jump over to the earth, to carry out his great deeds.

Now we have seen that Israel believes that God's word in general — and the prophetic word in particular — are the guiding and formative factor in its existence. This word makes Israel's history. From this it follows that the alignment with this word — the heeding of the prophetic preaching — is a necessity of life for Israel. In God's word his will to save is effected. If Israel listens to this word it is allowing itself to be taken up by God's will of salvation, and is carried further by it. If it resists however, God's word becomes a destructive sword: "Therefore," says God through Hosea, "I have hewn them by the prophets, I have slain them by the words of my mouth" (Hos. 6, 5).

God's **law** also has part in the enlivening power
of his word — for it also was given "out of the mouth
of the Lord" (Deut. 8, 3). The authentic-biblical
idea of God's law is none other than that it is the
word or **words** of God: "For this commandment
which I command you this day," says Moses to
Israel, "is not too hard for you, neither is it far off
. . . But the **word** is very near you; it is in your
mouth and in your heart, so that you can do it"
(Deut. 30, 11.14). Behind this text is the concept
of the word as a **force;** a force which is **in** the person, which wishes to figure in his actions. The word
of God's law also confronts mankind with a choice
between life and death: "I call heaven and earth to
witness against you this day, that I have set before
you life and death, blessing and curse; therefore
choose life, that you and your descendants may live,
loving the Lord your God, obeying his voice, and
cleaving to him" (Deut. 30, 19-20).

3

GOD'S WORD IN THE FULLNESS OF TIME

The letter to the Hebrews opens by connecting God's speaking to his people through the prophets in the Old Testament with his speaking to all humanity through Jesus Christ. This latter is the fulfillment of the former. This is God's word in the fullness of time — not only in the sense of coming "last of all, in these days" — but also in the sense that it completes, concludes, fulfills God's speaking in the Old Testament. The intention of the present chapter is to illustrate this general line of thought. Specific points of comparison between God's word in the Old and in the New Testament will be dealt with in later chapters as they arise.

Most important is the fact that the gospels portray Jesus as a **prophet.** In the preaching of the New Testament this is not the most characteristic aspect of Jesus' personality. However, it does typify his mission, placing it as a continuation of God's speaking in the Old Testament — which was above all a speaking through the prophets. The synoptic gospels (Matthew, Mark and Luke) describe the first acts of Jesus, and of his predecessor John the Baptist, as closely corresponding to those of the prophets. Their call to repentance (Mt. 3, 2; 4, 17; Mk. 1, 15) takes over a basic principle of the prophetic preaching. Their announcement "for the Kingdom of God is near" (idem.) is a deliberate calling to mind of the prophetic expectation of salvation.

Luke's solemn introduction to Jesus' public life (Lk. 3, 1-2) reminds one of the book of Ezekiel. It places John before us as a prophet, to whom God's word came, just as it came to the prophets — but then in a new age, in which "all flesh shall see the salvation of God" (Lk. 3, 6). This introduction, incidentally, is led up to in Luke's "childhood-gospel," in which he shows that the Forerunner (John) will be a prophet (cf. Lk. 1, 15; 17, 76-79). Also Jesus' first appearance in public, at Nazareth, is described by Luke as being typically that of a prophet — one who knows he is sent to preach the fulfillment of the ancient promises of salvation. Jesus applies to himself the words from Isaiah: "The Spirit of the Lord is upon me, because he has appointed me to preach good news to the poor . . ., to proclaim the acceptable year of the Lord" (Lk. 4, 18-19; compare Is. 61, 1-2).

Both John and Jesus make the impression on their contemporaries of being prophets, their mission appears to be directly connected with the messianic fulfillment: "Are you Elijah? . . . Are you the prophet?" they ask John (Jn. 1, 21). Regarding Jesus they say: "This is indeed the prophet who is to come into the world!" (Jn. 6, 14); and after his death:

". . . Jesus of Nazareth, who was a prophet mighty in word and deed before God and all the people" (Lk. 24, 19).

One point in the synoptic gospels places particular emphasis on Jesus' mission as a prophet. This is the Transfiguration, one of the heights in Jesus' life. The word of the Father: "This is my beloved Son, with whom I am well pleased; listen to him" (Mt. 17, 5) connects with Deuteronomy 18, 15 (cf. previous chapter); it shows that Jesus is the bearer of God's word, in whom the line of Moses and the prophets is culminated.

John's gospel also points out the prophetic nature of Jesus' mission, but this time the words reveal the deepest secret of his person. Jesus continually speaks here of himself as the **One Sent by God,** who tells of what he has seen and heard while with his Father: "For he whom God has sent utters the words of God, for it is not by measure that God gives the Spirit" (Jn. 3, 34). "He who sent me is true, and I declare to the world what I have heard from him" (Jn. 8, 26). The idea of sending, the close relationship between this idea and that of speaking-in-the-name-of-God, and the gift of the Spirit, these are all pointers toward prophecy. At the same time, however, these texts (and many others) of John's possess a depth, which is more profound than the mere notion of "prophet." They lead us into the mystery of the Only Begotten Son.

John condenses his own experience of the mystery of Christ, as he has seen and felt it, into a single term with immediate relationship to God's "speaking" in the Old Testament. The term "the Word" refers to Jesus Christ himself: "In the beginning was the Word, and the Word was with God, and the Word was God. . . . And the Word became flesh and dwelt among us" (Jn. 1, 1-14). The description is John's own invention; the term contains his entire thought regarding Jesus' person and mission. He is trying to make clear that all God's speaking in the Old Testament has achieved its highest culmination in the Only Begotten Son, who is come to bring salvation. God's creative word, his word of promise to the patriarchs, the prophetic word and the word of God's law, all of it becomes one in Jesus Christ; in him it becomes the source of life for a new humanity and a new world. He is "the Word of life" (1 Jn. 1, 1) in person, through whom God's salvation is to be fulfilled. "For the law was given through Moses; grace and truth came through Jesus Christ" (Jn. 1, 16-17). Grace and truth, the core and most valuable gift of God's speaking in the Old Testament, are achieved to the highest degree by Jesus Christ in his mission. That is why he is called "the Amen," the Seal on God's word (cf. Rev. 3, 14; 2 Cor. 1, 20).

In the New Testament, the preaching is based entirely on Jesus Christ, the Word. This alone is enough to characterize it as the fulfillment of God's word in the Old Testament. It also suggests to us why the New Testament is so uniquely rich and valuable.

4

JESUS, TEACHER AND WITNESS

Jesus Christ, the Word, speaks in the world in a human way — the word of God in human language. This is the great mission of his life. The salvation "was declared at first by the Lord" (Hebr. 2, 3). The new order, which he has come to establish, is centered in the **word** — a message of salvation. It begins with John the Baptist's preaching: "John the baptizer appeared in the wilderness, preaching a baptism of repentance for the forgiveness of sins" (Mk. 1, 4). Earliest Christendom has particularly applied two Old Testament texts to John — describing him as "the messenger" (Mal. 3, 1; cf. Mt. 11, 10) and "one crying in the wilderness" (Is. 40, 3; cf. Mt. 3, 3 etc.), announcing the approaching salvation.

The first we hear in the synoptic gospels of Jesus' public life is that he preaches: "Now after John was arrested, Jesus came into Galilee, preaching the gospel of God" (Mk. 1, 14). Then (after the baptism and the tempting): "Jesus returned in the power of the Spirit into Galilee, and a report concerning him went out through all the surrounding country. And he taught in their synagogues, being glorified by all" (Lk. 4, 14-15). On his listeners, he makes an impression of being a Teacher —

rather as the scribes were, but yet different: "And they were astonished at his teaching, for he taught them as one who had authority, and not as the scribes . . . And they were all amazed, so that they questioned among themselves, saying, 'What is this? A new teaching! With authority . . .'" (Mk. 1, 22-27). The people and his disciples prefer to address him with the title of the Jewish teachers: "Rabbi."

The continual teaching is in fact characteristic of Jesus' earthly life. It forms a theme — particularly in Mark's gospel — which keeps reappearing in the atmosphere of miracles, sympathy, misunderstanding and obstruction which surrounds the Master. "And they went into Capernaum; and immediately on the sabbath he entered the synagogue and taught" (Mk. 1, 21). "He went out again beside the sea; and all the crowd gathered about him, and he taught them" (Mk. 2, 13). "Again he began to teach beside the sea" (Mk. 4, 1). "And on the sabbath he began to teach in the synagogue" (Mk. 6, 2). "He went about among the villages teaching" (Mk. 6, 6). "As he landed he saw a great throng, and he had compassion on them, because they were like sheep without a shepherd; and he began to teach them many things" (Mk. 6, 34). "He left there and went to the region of Judea and beyond the Jordan, and crowds gathered to him again; and again, as his custom was, he taught them" (Mk. 10, 1). So it goes on. When he is arrested, Jesus condenses his entire public appearance in terms of the one word — "teaching." "Day after day I was with you

in the temple teaching, . . ." (Mk. 14, 49). Jesus
must teach; this is why he "came out" (Mk. 1, 38),
he "was sent for this purpose" (Lk. 4, 43).

At one point, Matthew gives a short review of
Jesus' work in Galilee — and he puts preaching in
the first place: "And he went about all Galilee,
teaching in their synagogues and preaching the
gospel of the Kingdom and healing every disease
and every infirmity among the people" (Mt. 4, 23;
also 9, 35). Later he quotes at some length from
the Old Testament, throwing light on Jesus' activity
as the gentle Teacher: "Behold, my Servant whom
I have chosen, my Beloved with whom my soul is
well pleased, I will put my spirit upon him, and he
shall proclaim justice to the Gentiles. He will not
wrangle or cry aloud, nor will any one hear his
voice in the streets; he will not break a bruised reed
or quench a smoldering wick, till he brings justice
to victory; and in his name will the Gentiles hope"
(Mt. 12, 18-21; from Is. 42, 1-4). This text shows the
thought of the evangelist, that Jesus — also by his
preaching — is **Christ:** the one who fulfills the written
word of the Old Testament. Indeed, Luke directly
connects the meaning of the term "Christ," "the
Anointed One," with Jesus' preaching: "The Spirit
of the Lord is upon me, because he has anointed me
to preach good news to the poor" (Lk. 4, 18). This
quotation from Is. 61, which Jesus applies to himself, speaks of an **anointing** with the Spirit of God
for the proclamation of God's salvation. This spiritual
anointment, which implies a power (cf. Lk. 4, 14;

also Acts 10, 38), has incidentally another effect — it gives Jesus the ability to perform miracles. This will be discussed in a later chapter.

What the synoptic gospels tell us about Jesus' activity as a teacher is also to be found in John's gospel — but in other words, illuminated as it were from another angle. John also begins the new order of salvation with the preaching by John the Baptist, but he treats it as a **testimony** of Jesus: "There was a man sent from God, whose name was John. He came for testimony, to bear witness to the light . . ." (Jn. 1, 6-7). This testimony resounds through all times: "John bore witness to him, and cried: This was he of whom I said, 'He who comes after me ranks before me, for he was before me'" (Jn. 1, 15). Regarding Jesus himself, the evangelist John at first emphasizes the revelation of his glory and power by signs and by his appearance at Jerusalem (cf. Jn. 2 and 4, 46-54); this remains one of the main themes of his gospel. Besides this however an important part of John's gospel is a reproduction of Jesus' words — and "speaking" is for Jesus no less characteristic than the performing of miracles. "If I had not come and spoken to them, they would not have sin; but now they have no excuse for their sin" (Jn. 15, 22). Jesus declares before his judges: "I have spoken openly to the world; I have always taught in synagogues and in the temple, where all Jews come together; I have said nothing secretly. Why do you ask me? Ask those who have heard me, what I said to them; they know what I said"

(Jn. 18, 20-21). This is John's parallel text for Jesus' declaration in Gethsemane, Mk. 14, 49. The officers of the Sanhedrin echo the impression Jesus made on his contemporaries: "No man ever spoke like this man!" (Jn. 7, 46).

Jesus' speaking in John's gospel is in essence that of the One Sent, as was pointed out in the previous chapter. For that reason it is a speaking in the name of the Father: ". . . I . . . speak thus as the Father taught me" (Jn. 8, 28). The first part of the gospel closes on this theme: "For I have not spoken on my own authority; the Father who sent me has himself given me commandment what to say and what to speak. And I know that his commandment is eternal life. What I say, therefore, I say as the Father has bidden me" (Jn. 12, 49-50).

John's gospel is also unique in its use of the word "testimony" to describe Jesus' speaking during his earthly life. This testimony points out the secret of his person, like the sending theme. Jesus bears witness, because he speaks out of his intimacy with God, his Father, about what he has heard and seen while with the Father: "No one has ever seen God; the only Son, who is in the bosom of the Father, he has made him known" (Jn. 1, 18). "He bears witness to what he has seen and heard, yet no one receives his testimony" (Jn. 3, 32). Jesus himself says: "Truly, truly, I say to you, we speak of what we know, and bear witness to what we have seen" (Jn. 3, 11). "For this I was born, and for this I have

come into the world, to bear witness to the truth"
(Jn. 18, 37).

This is the beginning of salvation in the fullness
of time; Jesus Christ speaks, as Teacher and as
Witness of the Father. This is the thought with which
Peter opens his preaching to the Gentiles: "You
know the word which he (God) sent to Israel,
preaching good news of peace by Jesus Christ"
(Acts 10, 36).

5

THE ONES WHO WERE SENT

The Choice and the Commission

After the salvation "was declared at first by the Lord, . . . it was attested to us by those who heard him" (Hebr. 2, 3). These words give the New Testament concept of the path of salvation in the world. Started by the speaking of Our Lord, it is spread further by those who pass on in "an attested way" what they have heard from him.

All the gospels, even as they start to describe Jesus' public life, raise the expectation of his work of salvation being continued — by a group of men chosen by him. The choice of several disciples is mentioned by Matthew and Mark directly after their account of Jesus' first appearance (Mt. 4, 18-22; Mk. 1, 16-20). John places his description before that of the first miracle at Cana (Jn. 1, 35-51). Later, the three synoptic gospels tell the story of the calling of Matthew (Mt. 2, 14 etc.). They also give Jesus' promise to those first called, that he will make them fishers of men (cf. also Lk. 5, 10). With this specific promise, Jesus places himself above the Jewish rabbis. Not only does he collect disciples around himself — he is also conscious of a mission of salvation for mankind, which he must pass on.

Another moment is the choice of the Twelve, described by Mark and Luke. The context shows Jesus at one of the heights of his ministry: "Jesus withdrew with his disciples to the sea, and a great multitude from Galilee followed; also from Judea and Jerusalem and Idumea and from beyond the Jordan and from about Tyre and Sidon a great multitude, hearing all that he did, came to him. And he told his disciples to have a boat ready for him because of the crowd, lest they should crush him; for he had healed many, so that all who had diseases pressed upon him to touch him. And whenever the unclean spirits beheld him, they fell down before him and cried out, 'You are the Son of God.' And he strictly ordered them not to make him known. And he went up into the hills, and called to him those whom he desired; and they came to him. And he appointed twelve, to be with him, and to be sent out to preach and have authority to cast out demons." Then there follow the names of the Twelve (Mk. 3, 7-19; cf. also Lk. 6, 12-19). It is possibly of some significance that the episode follows a series of conflicts with the scribes and pharisees, which end with the plan to bring Jesus to death (Mk. 2, 1-3, 6) — the Master is already laying the foundations for the continuation of his work after his death. In evangelical tradition, the choice of the Twelve is inseparable from the concept of **sending** or **mission.** "And he appointed twelve . . . to be sent out to preach" (Mk. 3, 14). Where Matthew and Luke give a review of the Twelve, they call them "apostles" — which means "persons who have been

dominated by a theme characteristic of Jesus' speaking in this gospel. The theme is: what the Son has received from the Father, he passes on to mankind. This can be seen in the way he tells the apostles about the words and commission which he was given by the Father: "No longer do I call you servants, for the servant does not know what his master is doing; but I have called you friends, for all that I have heard from my Father I have made known to you" (Jn. 15, 15). In the pontifical prayer, Jesus speaks to the Father: "For I have given them the words which thou gavest me. . . . As thou didst send me into the world, so I have sent them into the world. . . . I do not pray for these only, but also for those who believe in me through their word" (Jn. 17, 8. 18. 20). Then comes the commission itself; the Risen One says: "As the Father has sent me, even so I send you" (Jn. 20, 21). Jesus has told the apostles the Father's secrets (cf. Jn. 15, 15); now they are his witnesses, just as he is the Father's witness (cf. Jn. 15, 27).

The Path of the Word

After the ascension of Jesus and the descent of the Holy Spirit the word is carried through the world by the preaching of the missionaries, the ones who were sent. The second story written by Luke, the Acts of the Apostles, has this path of the word — in the power of the Holy Spirit — as its central theme. The Twelve are at first centrally placed; they were sent out by Jesus directly and they are eye-witnesses of his life and of the risen Lord. Being

witnesses and giving testimony is their entirely
unique vocation. This is the motivation for the
choice of Mathias in the place of Judas. Peter
puts it this way: "So one of the men who have
accompanied us during all the time that the Lord
Jesus went in and out among us, beginning from
the baptism of John until the day when he was
taken up from us — one of these men must become
with us a witness to his resurrection" (Acts 1, 21-22).
Regularly they state their testimony; for example,
Peter at the Pentecost feast: "This Jesus God raised
up, and of that we are all witnesses" (Acts 2, 32).
Testimony is a characteristic of their appearances:
"And with great power the apostles gave their
testimony to the resurrection of the Lord Jesus"
(Acts 4, 33). They are "those who from the beginning
were eye-witnesses" (Lk. 1, 2). This witness is in the
service of the preaching of salvation. Luke gives a
few typical examples of this preaching, indeed he
depicts them above all as preachers: "And every day
in the temple and at home they did not cease
teaching and preaching Jesus as the Christ" (Acts
5, 42). Preaching is their most important task: "It
is not right," say the Twelve to the assembled
faithful, "that we should give up preaching the word
of God to serve tables. . . . But we will devote ourselves to prayer and to the ministry of the word"
(Acts 6, 2. 4). They **must** preach: "For we cannot
but speak of what we have seen and heard" (Acts
4, 20).

Luke shows how the word finds its way from
Jerusalem. After the stoning of Stephen the first

breakthrough of Israel's borders is made: "Now
those who were scattered (by the persecution) went
about preaching the word. Philip went down to
a city of Samaria, and proclaimed to them the
Christ" (Acts 8, 4-5). After Peter — on a sign from
God — has baptized the first group of pagans
(Acts 10), the description is given of the real start
of the mission to the pagans in Antioch. The first
impulse comes once again from those who had dis-
persed after the death of Stephen (Acts 11, 19-20).
This forms a bridge-passage in the book, leading to
the second part, which deals with Paul's preaching
(13-28). Luke portrays Paul as the one through
whom Jesus' word, spoken before the ascension, will
be fulfilled — at least as far as the last part is concerned: "You shall be my witnesses in Jerusalem and
in all Judea and Samaria **and to the end of the
earth**" (Acts 1, 8). Paul is repeatedly called a **witness**
of the risen Christ, whom he saw near Damascus
(cf. Acts 9). This is important. Paul knows he was
sent by the risen Lord, just like the Twelve. Luke
therefore gives him the title of apostle, the same
as Barnabas (Acts 14, 4. 14). Paul shows that he
appreciates his witness and mission, when he relates to king Agrippa what happened to him near
Damascus: "And the Lord said: 'I am Jesus whom
you are persecuting. But rise and stand upon your
feet; for I have appeared to you for this purpose,
to appoint you to serve and bear witness to the
things in which you have seen me and to those
in which I will appear to you, delivering you from
the people (Israel) and from the Gentiles — to whom

I send you to open their eyes . . .'" (Acts 26, 15-18).
Luke shows us Paul, just like the Twelve, as
preaching continually. The first and the last we
hear of him, he is preaching. After his conversion
"he was (for several days) with the disciples at
Damascus. And in the synagogues immediately he
proclaimed Jesus, saying: 'He is the Son of God'"
(Acts 9, 20). "And he lived there two whole years
at his own expense, and welcomed all who came
to him, preaching the kingdom of God and teaching
about the Lord Jesus Christ quite openly and unhindered" (Acts 28, 30-31). These texts can be com-
plemented with innumerable statements taken from
his letters. The following, taken as an example,
beautifully illustrates the secret of Paul's apostolate:
"But when he who had set me apart before I was
born, and had called me through his grace, was
pleased to reveal his Son to me, in order that I might
preach him among the Gentiles. . . ." (Gal. 1, 15-16).
Another text contains his entire appreciation of his
task: "For Christ did not send me to baptize but to
preach the gospel" (1 Cor. 1, 17). Shortly before
his imprisonment he can testify: ". . . from Jerusalem
and as far round as Illyricum I have fully preached
the gospel of Christ" (Rom. 15, 19).

Alongside the Twelve and Paul, and dependent
upon them, we see innumerable others busy preaching the word — such as the Seven (cf. Acts 6, 5-6) of
whom Stephen (cf. Acts 6, 8-15; & 7) and Philip
(cf. Acts 8, 1-8; 26-40) are noteworthy. Paul calls
these helpers his fellow-workers and fellow-soldiers

(Rom. 16, 21; Phil. 2, 25). Among the **charismata** or gifts of intellect — and these were frequent in apostolic times — the principal ones relate to the word: "And his (Christ's) gifts were that some should be apostles, some prophets, some evangelists, some pastors and teachers" (Eph. 4, 11).

Servants of the Lord

Since the apostles were sent out on their mission by Christ, they are his servants: "Truly, truly, I say to you, a servant is not greater than his master; nor is he who is sent greater than he who sent him" (Jn. 13, 16). Paul refers to himself and to his helpers as servants (or slaves) of God and Christ: "Paul and Timothy, servants of Christ Jesus" (Phil. 1, 1). He also speaks of his "fellow servants" (Col. 1, 7). Still more frequently we meet the Greek term **diakonos** which has led to our word "deacon"; it was first applied to the Seven (Acts 6, 1-6), meaning minister or servant rather than slave. Paul also applies this term to himself and to the other preachers, as being servants of God, of Christ: "Timothy, our brother and God's servant in the gospel of Christ" (1 Thess. 3, 2). He also connects the title with his mission, speaking of himself and his helpers as: "ministers of a new covenant, not in a written code but in the Spirit" (2 Cor. 3, 6). Also: "Of this gospel I was made a minister" (Eph. 3, 7) and: ". . . the church, of which I became a minister . . ." (Col. 1, 25). The apostolate itself is frequently referred to as a ministry: ". . . the ministry of the word" (Acts 6, 4). ". . . God, who through Christ reconciled us to himself and gave us the ministry of reconciliation" (2 Cor. 5, 18). Another Greek term occurs, which has been translated with "minister" and "servant"; more correctly it means "helper": "They . . . who from the beginning were eye-witnesses and ministers (helpers) of the word" (Lk. 1, 2). "This is how one should regard us, as servants (helpers) of Christ and stewards of the mysteries of God" (1 Cor. 4, 1).

Paul also sees the apostolate as a priestly service, a liturgy: ". . . the grace given me by God to be a minister of Christ Jesus to the Gentiles in the priestly service of the gospel of God, so that the offering of the Gentiles may be acceptable, sanctified by the Holy Spirit" (Rom. 15, 15-16). Similarly: "God . . . whom I serve with my spirit in the gospel of his Son" (Rom. 1, 9). The preachers are also represented as laborers at God's and Christ's harvest: "I sent you" says Jesus to the apostles "to reap that for which you did not labor; others have labored, and you have entered into their labor" (Jn. 4, 38; cf. also Mt. 9, 37-38). They are planters in the service of God: "What then is Apollos? What is Paul? Servants through whom you believed, as the Lord assigned to each. I planted, Apollos watered, but God gave the growth. . . . For we are fellow workers for God; you are God's field, God's building" (1 Cor. 3, 5-9).

The "ones who were sent" are therefore completely involved with the Lord and his work. For that reason they speak in commission and name of the Lord. They are to be respected as the person of the Lord and as the heavenly Father himself. Jesus declares to his apostles: "He who receives you receives me, and he who receives me receives him who sent me" (Mt. 10, 40). "He who hears you hears me, and he who rejects you rejects me, and he who rejects me rejects him who sent me" (Lk. 10, 16). "Truly, truly, I say to you, he who receives any one whom I send receives me; and he who receives me receives him who sent me" (Jn. 13, 20). In these three texts it is the **mission** which gives the preachers more than human pretensions. Their word is therefore also that of God and of Christ: "And we also thank God constantly for this, that when you received the word of God which you heard from us, you accepted it not as the word of men but as what it really is, the word of God, which is at work in you believers" (1 Thess. 2, 13). Paul is aware of the fact that it is Christ in him who speaks (cf. 2 Cor. 13, 3). "So we are ambassadors for Christ, God making his appeal through us. We beseech you on behalf of Christ, be reconciled to God" (2 Cor. 5, 20). In this appreciation he actually identifies himself and Barnabas with the Messiah, the light of the Gentiles, when he introduces an Old Testament prophecy about the Servant of Yahweh, the Lord: "For so the Lord has commanded **us,** saying: 'I have set you to be a light for the Gentiles, that you may bring salvation to the uttermost parts of the earth'" (Acts 13, 47).

This unity between Christ and the preachers is also implied in the following passage from the letter to the Romans: "But how are men to call upon him

(Christ) in whom they have not believed? And how
are they to believe in him of whom they have never
heard? And how are they to hear without a
preacher?" (Rom. 10, 14). He who comes to Christ
through belief must first of all have heard him. But
one hears him in the preacher — who is therefore
not merely speaking **about** Christ, but rather in and
through whom Christ himself is actually speaking.
"What I also delivered to you . . ."

The path of the word is not only a spreading out
from Jerusalem to the end of the earth. It consists
also in a descending from Christ into the heart of
the person who believes. The steps in this aspect
of the path, from the heights to down below, are
summed up in the text just quoted (1 Thess. 2, 13).
They are the preaching, the reception of the preaching by listening to it, the acceptance of the word
and, finally, the believing. The first stages in this
process, the preaching itself and the listening to it,
are pointed out in the New Testament by the use
of two specific terms — both of which deal with
the preaching in the objective sense. We come
across the "delivery" and the "reception" of doctrines
or commandments, of "traditions." "Delivery" in this
usage means "handing down," "traditions" are things
(beliefs, customs etc.) handed down. How closely
these two terms are associated is to be seen from
the forms of the Greek verbs concerned; we could
translate them literally as "giving over" and "taking
over." We already meet the combination of both
in quite early texts of the New Testament, for

example: "Now we command you, brethren, in the name of our Lord Jesus Christ, that you keep away from any brother who is living in idleness and not in accord with the **tradition** that you **received** from us" (2 Thess. 3, 6); and again, in the very important texts of the first letter to the Corinthians: "For I **received** from the Lord what I also **delivered** to you, that the Lord Jesus on the night when he was betrayed took bread, and when he had given thanks, he broke it, and said: 'This is my body which is for you. Do this in remembrance of me'" (1 Cor. 11, 23-24). "Now I would remind you, brethren, in what terms I preached to you the gospel, which you **received,** in which you stand, by which you are saved, if you hold fast — unless you believed in vain. For I **delivered** to you as of first importance what I also **received,** that Christ died for our sins in accordance with the scriptures" (1 Cor. 15, 1-4).

In the last two texts, Paul himself is the one who first "received" — in order to later "hand down." In 1 Cor. 11, 23 the source from which he received is very specifically the Lord. Nothing prevents us however, from considering the milieu of the apostolic church — and specifically the Twelve — as being the immediate source of this tradition. This is indeed the only possible interpretation of the text of 1 Cor. 15, 1-4 if we bear the following passages in mind. The main and essential point is that the belief of the Christian community must be based on tradition, if it is to lead to salvation; one must hold fast to the gospel as it is handed down (cf. 1

Cor. 15, 2). This authoritative and norm-setting character of the tradition is one of its most noteworthy aspects: "So then, brethren, stand firm and hold to the traditions which you were taught by us, either by word of mouth or by letter" (2 Thess. 2, 15). "If any one is preaching to you a gospel contrary to that which you received, let him be accursed" (Gal. 1, 9). "I commend you because you remember me in everything and maintain the traditions even as I have delivered them to you" (1 Cor. 11, 2). "As therefore you received Christ Jesus the Lord, so live in him" (Col. 2, 6). Jude, the brother of James, writes: "Beloved, . . . I found it necessary to write appealing to you to contend for the faith which was once for all delivered to the saints" (Jude 3).

The New Testament sees the preaching of the word, in spite of its richness and variety, as a clearly outlined and unchallangeable quantity. It is a "tradition," which comes from the Lord, and which is handed down by his eye-witnesses (cf. Lk. 1, 2). Received by their listeners, it must be held fast as it was received and accepted.

Paul's last letters, to Timothy and Titus, are inspired by just that care for the true maintenance of this tradition, this good, this "sound doctrine." He writes: "But as for you, teach what befits sound doctrine" (Tit. 2, 1). ". . . continue in what you have learned and have firmly believed" (2 Tim. 3, 14). Paul speaks of the truths which have been entrusted: "And therefore I suffer as I do. But I am not ashamed, for I know whom I have believed, and I

am sure that he is able to guard until that Day
what has been entrusted to me. Follow the pattern
of the sound words which you have heard from me,
in the faith and love which are in Christ Jesus; guard
the truth that has been entrusted to you by the
Holy Spirit who dwells within us" (2 Tim. 1, 12-14).
The theme of this text follows the same line as that
regarding the handing down; the Lord entrusted
Paul with truth, which he has passed on to others
— now he urges them to hold fast to it. The word
"entrusted," with the sense of "given in deposit,"
lays strong emphasis on the unchallengeable and
inalienable nature of the truths. Paul earnestly
warns his disciple: "O Timothy, guard what has
been entrusted to you" (1 Tim. 6, 20). At the same
time however, he speaks of "handing down" the
"deposit" to following generations: "You then, my
son, be strong in the grace that is in Christ Jesus, and
what you have heard from me before many witnesses
(a reference to Timothy's baptism or ordination)
entrust to faithful men who will be able to teach
others also" (2 Tim. 2, 1-2). It is obviously vital
that the Christian community should carry the sound
doctrine — unalloyed and undiminished — with it
through the centuries.

Until the end of time

Paul's horizon is defined by "the Day," the day
of Christ's appearance in majesty. He himself hopes
to keep — by the power of Christ — the entrusted
truths safe "until that Day" (2 Tim. 1, 12). His last
passionate appeal to Timothy is prefaced by a

reference to the great Day: "I charge you in the presence of God and of Christ Jesus who is to judge the living and the dead, and by his appearing and his kingdom: preach the word, be urgent in season and out of season, convince, rebuke, and exhort, be unfailing in patience and in teaching. . . Do the work of an evangelist, fulfill your ministry" (2 Tim. 4, 1-5). How will the coming generations guard the deposit of sound doctrine? Paul points to the power of the Holy Spirit: "Guard the truth that has been entrusted to you by the Holy Spirit who dwells within us" (2 Tim. 1, 14). This is in essence the same thought as that contained in Jesus' promise, as he sends out the Eleven: "Go therefore and make disciples of all nations . . . I am with you always, to the close of the age" (Mt. 28, 19-20).

The continuing presence of the Lord ensures that his command will be faithfully carried out. The text from Matthew assumes that the apostles' preaching will be continued until the end of time. Just how this will be done is not given. As in all biblical texts dealing with the distant future, the perspective remains vague. What is shown clearly is how the **handing down of the apostolic mission** takes place. The appointment of the Seven (Acts 6, 1-7) is related to the preaching. Certainly, they are at first intended to administer the distribution of the material goods of charity (the word "deacon" means this); but it cannot be just coincidence that we later read only about their (specifically Stephen's and Philip's) preaching. The latter was known as "the evangelist"

(cf. Acts 21, 8). Paul and Barnabas were the ones
sent directly by the Holy Spirit to preach among
the Gentiles (cf. Acts 13, 1-4); yet one could ask
oneself if the laying on of hands, mentioned in the
Acts 6, 1-7, is not also a **commission.** Considered
this way, "they laid their hands upon them" shows
the Christian community of Antioch — one in spirit
with its leaders — taking on the mission of the Holy
Spirit, and commending the missionaries "to the
grace of God" (cf. Acts 14, 26).

We already quoted this passage from Paul's writings: "But how are men to call upon him (Christ)
in whom they have not believed? And how are
they to believe in him of whom they have never
heard? And how are they to hear without a
preacher? **And how can men preach unless they are
sent?"** (Rom. 10, 14-15). Perhaps Paul is thinking
mainly of the apostles here, perhaps not. His formulation is however general, appearing to mean:
preaching is never possible without a mission. If we
assume that the preaching in the Church must
continue, then the mission of the apostles must be
passed on to others. To Archippus, whom Paul calls
his fellow soldier (Philemon 2), he sends the message: "See that you fulfill the ministry which you
have received in the Lord" (Col. 4, 17). The term
used here for "received" is the same as that used
elsewhere for the "receiving" of the doctrine. In
the same way as the doctrine is handed down by
the first leaders of the Church, there is clearly also
a handing down of the ministry by these leaders —

i.e. a **sending.** If we consider what we have already generally found the meaning of the word "ministry" to be, we can assume that here too the sending, the mission, will be to **preach.**

There is a difficult question which we cannot discuss here, the relationship between the gifts of intellect (charismata) and the corresponding "office" in the earliest Christian community. We are specifically concerned here with the concept of preaching, as gift and as office. That there was such a thing as an office in apostolic times in general, is a fact. This is shown by the way, for example, in which the apostles appointed elders to be leaders of the newly founded communities (cf. Acts 14, 23), and by the actual presence of such leaders (cf. Acts 15; Phil. 1, 1; Hebr. 13, 7). Paul instructs Titus to appoint, in his turn, elders in every town (Tit. 1, 5). These really have a function as leaders and also as teachers (cf. 1 Tim. 5, 17). The concept of an **office** of preaching, based on a **mission** which certain men receive from the apostles — and which they will later hand down to others — is fully compatible with this structure.

Titus himself and Timothy are definite examples of such a mission. Paul speaks to Timothy regarding his appointment by laying on of hands: "Do not neglect the gift you have, which was given you by prophetic utterance when the elders laid their hands upon you" (1 Tim. 4, 14), and ". . . the laying on of my hands (2 Tim. 1, 6). The context of these quotations is closely connected with Paul's concern for the safe keeping of the sound doctrine; this is a major theme of his letters to Timothy and Titus. Holding this doctrine before the communities' attention and helping it to make an impression is an important part of their task: "Take heed to yourself and to your teaching; hold to that, for by so doing you will save both yourself and your hearers" (1 Tim. 4, 16).

So Paul instructs Timothy to pass on the doctrine, which he has received, to trustworthy men who in their own turn will be able to instruct still others (2 Tim. 2, 2). This is the beginning of a progression of missionaries, ones who are sent, who will guard and maintain the "entrusted truths" until that Day, the end of time.

6

THE MEANING OF THE PREACHING

The word spoken by Jesus and by those whom he sends, is at once a message sent by God and a doctrine regarding the path to salvation. Before analyzing these two aspects we will discuss the **meaning** of the preaching. We will do this by looking at the terms used to describe the preaching in the New Testament. The precise background of these terms, given by the Bible, reveals its thinking on this subject.

Speaking

The words regarding preaching used in the New Testament are more varied than those of the Old; the appearance of the prophets there is usually referred to as "speaking," their message as "the word of the Lord" or "the word of the Lord God." The New Testament takes over this method of expression. It lives on in the regularly recurring "I say to you" of Jesus and in the description of his and the apostles' preaching as "the word of God" or simply, "the word." Their preaching is also frequently called "speaking," particularly in Luke's writings. This speaking however has a new content, a new meaning: "He (Jesus) . . . spoke to them about the **Kingdom of God**" (Lk. 9, . 11). Paul asks for prayers, that it may be given to him to speak of "the **mystery of Christ**" (Col. 4, 3). The preaching of the New Testament is called the word of Christ, the word of the Lord, the word of grace, of the good news, of the Kingdom, of salvation, of the cross.

In the use of the term "speaking," "God's word," by the New Testament lies a new indication of the **prophetic character** of the preaching. The missionaries of the New Testament are — no less than the prophets — speakers in the name of God. Their words too are charged with God's power. Their mission too is in the service of the communication between God and his people, the Covenant. This latter thought has inspired Paul to write a moving passage about the glorious nature of the ministry of the word in the New Testament: "Such is the confidence that we have through Christ toward God. Not that we are sufficient of ourselves to claim anything as coming from us; our sufficiency is from God, who has qualified us to be ministers of a new covenant, not in a written code but in the Spirit; for the written code kills, but the Spirit gives life. Now if the dispensation of death, carved in letters on stone, came with such splendor that the Israelites could not look at Moses' face because of its brightness, fading as this was, will not the dispensation of the Spirit be attended with greater splendor? . . . For if what faded away came with splendor, what is permanent must have much more splendor (2 Cor. 3, 4-11). The Christian, Christ's missionary, reflects in the first place the glory, the splendor, of the Lord himself: "And we all, with unveiled face, beholding the glory of the Lord, are being changed into his likeness from one degree of glory to another; for this comes from the Lord who is the Spirit" (2 Cor. 3, 18).

John takes, as usual, a unique position. In his gospel, speaking is the standard expression for Jesus' preaching, to the exclusion of all other terms except "teaching." This speaking is very closely connected with the dominant theme of the sending of Jesus by the Father.

In general, we can say that speaking, as a synonym for preaching occurs less frequently in the New Testament than two other expressions: "declare" (or "proclaim"), and the "bringing of good news."

Proclamation, declaration

The Greek verb which is here rendered with "to proclaim" or "to declare" is properly applied to the public herald or town crier; in the past the herald would loudly make known in public some happening, ruling etc. "Proclaim" is therefore really the better rendering in our language. This is the sense in which those who were healed proclaim to all what Jesus has done for them (Mk. 1, 45; 5, 20; 7, 36). Most frequently in the New Testament, however, the word relates to the preaching by Jesus or the apostles. The Old Testament (in the Greek translation) applied the word to the prophetic preaching:

"The Spirit of the Lord God is upon me, because the Lord has anointed me to bring good tidings to the afflicted; he has sent me to bind up the broken-hearted, to **proclaim** liberty to the captives, and the opening of the prison to those who are bound; to **proclaim** the year of the Lord's favor, . . ." (Is. 61, 1-2). "Blow the trumpet in Zion; **sound the alarm** on my holy mountain! Let all the inhabitants of the land tremble, for the day of the Lord is coming, it is near" (Joel 2, 1).

Texts like these are already moving into the atmosphere of the New Testament. The New Testament is dealing with a proclamation, the announcement of a great new happening — the coming of God's salvation, of his Kingdom. The term is particularly well applied, therefore, when it deals with a **first** appearance of Jesus or one of the other preachers: "John the baptizer appeared in the wilderness, proclaiming* a baptism of repentance for the forgiveness of sins" (Mk. 1, 4). "Now after John was arrested, Jesus came into Galilee, proclaiming* the gospel of God" (Mk. 1, 14). "And he went about all Galilee, teaching in their synagogues and proclaiming* the gospel of the Kingdom" (Mt. 4, 23). Jesus' first commission to the Twelve reads: "And preach as you go, declaring*: 'The Kingdom of Heaven is at hand'" (Mt. 10, 7). After his resurrection: "Go into all the world, proclaiming* the gospel to the whole creation" (Mk. 16, 15). Paul writes to the Thessalonians: "For you remember our labor and toil, brethren; we worked night and day, that

we might not burden any of you, while we proclaimed* to you the gospel of God" (1 Thess. 2, 9).

Alongside the new and surprising aspects, the
idea of **public announcement** remains associated with
the term. This is shown in the text of Mark 16, 15
above. It appears also very clearly in this from
Matthew: "What I tell you in the dark, utter in the
light; and what you hear whispered, **proclaim** upon
the **housetops**" (Mt. 10, 27). Paul also applies the
title "herald" to himself: "For this gospel I was
appointed a **herald,** an apostle and teacher" (2 Tim.
1.11; cf. also 1 Tim. 2, 7 and translator's note below).

In John's gospel we do not find the same original
for "proclaim" (although this word is occasionally
used in the Revised Standard Version of John's work).
John puts the same idea across with a word meaning
"cry out" or "call," applied to the witnesses of God;
"John (the baptizer) bore witness to him (Jesus),
and **cried** . . ." (Jn. 1, 15). 'So Jesus proclaimed, as
he taught in the temple . . ." (Jn. 7, 28). "And Jesus
cried out and said: 'He who believes in me, believes
not in me but in him who sent me'" (Jn. 12, 44).
All gospels describe John as the "voice of one **crying**
in the wilderness" (cf. e.g. Lk. 3, 4).

The public nature of the preaching — it can be
heard by all — is also rendered in other ways. At
Pentecost, "Peter, standing with the eleven, **lifted**

————
*Translator's Note: These departures from the Revised Stand-
  ard Version are necessary to enable the writer's point —
regarding the Greek text — to be made.

up his voice and addressed them. . . ." (Acts 2, 14). The high priest accuses the apostles: "You have filled Jerusalem with your teaching" (Acts 5, 28). Paul testifies to the elders of Ephesus that he has omitted nothing useful to them, while declaring and teaching them "in public and from house to house" (Acts 20, 20).

Good news

Another characteristic aspect of New Testament language is a verb which can only be rendered by the phrase "preach good news." There is a stronger connection with the Old Testament here than there is, for example, with the proclaim concept; and the evangelists point out that it was Jesus himself who established it. At his first appearance (in the synagogue) in Nazareth, Jesus applies the Isaiah text to himself, a text containing the good news (cf. Lk. 4, 16-19). Jesus again refers to this text, in his answer to the imprisoned John the Baptist's disciples: "Go and tell John what you hear and see: the blind receive their sight and the lame walk, . . . and the poor have good news preached to them" (Mt. 11, 4-5). It would appear that Jesus deliberately took over the good news concept from the Old Testament, to characterize his preaching. The concept carries with it the entire context of the second part of the book of Isaiah (40-66), in which the preaching of the good news is the prophetic announcement of Israel's release and recovery after the Babylonian captivity (cf. Is. 40, 9; 52, 7; 60, 6). The prophet speaking here treats this as **the** salvation, the messianic salvation. When it was applied to Jesus' preaching, therefore, the expression gave the listeners a clear suggestion of the messianic nature of his appearance and of the fulfillment of the prophecies.

The concept of good news, we see therefore, was applied directly by Jesus to the New Testament preaching. Among the New Testament writers, Luke and Paul have a distinct preference for the specific verb. The noun for good news (**euangelion**) from which comes our "evangel" (gospel) — carries the stamp of Paul. The apostle's preference for the word comes no doubt, at least in part, from the influence of the Greek culture on the Graeco-Roman world of his time. The person of the emperor was an object of religious veneration; his great days (birth, coronation, arrival in town etc.) were good news for the people. The person of Christ the Lord, with **his** great days (death, resurrection, glorification, coming at the end of time), was — for Paul — the source of **the euangelion,** the only good news. In the New Testament the term can apply to the preaching itself or to its content, but not to the writing; our usage of "evangelic" as the adjective belonging to "gospel" is **more recent** than apostolic times.

Looking further, we find the idea of "message" or "tidings," applied in the form of four verbs to the preaching. Luke uses these in the Acts to some extent, but they occur far less frequently than the others.

In John's writing the concept of good news in the above sense is entirely absent. The reason for this is that John sees the Church's preaching less as a message of coming salvation than as a witness of a living reality — the Son of God, made man and glorified: "That which was from the beginning, which we have heard, which we have seen with our eyes, which we have looked upon and touched with our hands, concerning the word of life — the life was made manifest, and we saw it, and testify to it, and proclaim to you the eternal life which was the Father and was made manifest to us — that which we have seen and heard we proclaim also to you . . ." (1 John 1, 1-3). John speaks of "proclaiming," but not with the typical term (see earlier) which is so usual elsewhere in the New Testament. For him the foreground is the living experience of the Word of Life, to which he bears witness.

Proclamation and good news incidentally are closely related to each other. We see this in the frequent occurrence of the phrase "proclaim the good news" — given frequently in the Revised Standard Version as "preach the gospel." The meaning is identical. The use of these terms in the New Testament spotlights the aspects "new" and "amazing," "salvation-bringing" and "accessible for all" of the preaching, while still showing that it is the fulfillment of the prophecies.

Doctrine

Besides the expressions we have dealt with up to now, the noun "doctrine" or "teaching" with the verb "to teach" ("indoctrinate" means something else!) has an important place in New Testament language.

The gospels and the Acts, above all, frequently describe Jesus and the apostles as "teachers." In general, this teaching is closely connected with preaching the gospel, with proclaiming the good news. It comes in the same texts: "When Jesus had finished instructing his twelve disciples, he went on from there to teach and preach in their cities" (Mt. 11, 1). "Every day in the temple and at home they did not cease teaching and preaching Jesus as the Christ" (Acts 5, 42). The phrase "teach . . . in the name of Jesus" (Acts 4, 18) also brings "teach" close to "proclaim" and "good news."

Teaching is not however synonymous with preaching. The most obvious difference is that teaching is a longer process, something Jesus "sits down" to (cf. Mt. 5, 2; Lk. 5, 3). The Greek form makes this plain by using the imperfect or continuous past tense of the verb. Teaching can be carried on through several occasions for one audience: "Day after day I sat in the temple teaching, and you did not seize me" (Mt. 26, 55). To put it generally, teaching is an expanding and explaining of what has already been preached (proclaimed). The actual content of the teaching or doctrine will be worked out in a later chapter.

All we can do here is to give the function of teaching as opposed to proclaiming some general attention. In the same way as for the other terms we will take a look at the Old Testament. "Teaching" means here holding up God's will and law before Israel, with its basis in the Covenant, to bring the people to an attitude of obedience and holy awe for the Lord. Moses speaks in Deuteronomy: "And now, O Israel, give heed to the statutes and the ordinances which I teach you, and do them; that you may live, and go in and take possession of the land. . . . On the day that you stood before the Lord your God at Horeb, the Lord said to me: 'Gather the people to me, that I may let them hear my words, so that they may **learn** to fear me all the days that they live upon the earth, and that they may **teach** their children so' . . . And he declared to you his covenant, which he commanded you to perform, that is, the ten commandments; and he wrote them upon two tables of stone" (Deut. 4, 1-10; 13). The individual in the Old Testament understands "learning" in a religious sense as being the forming of his entire way of life, according to God's will in the Covenant. He prays about this: "Make me to know thy ways, O Lord, teach me thy paths. Lead me in thy truth, and teach me, for thou art the God of my salvation. . . " (Ps. 25, 4-5).

The preaching of Jesus and the apostles is also a teaching in this sense, insofar as they inform their hearers about God's will of salvation. He wishes a communion with mankind, in the form of a New Covenant, from which an entirely new way of life can be built up for mankind. It is the fulfillment of what Jeremiah prophesied: "I will put my law within them, and I will write it upon their hearts; and I will be their God, and they shall be my people" (Jer. 31, 33). In John's gospel we find an indication of the connection between the "teaching" in the New Testament and God's will: "So Jesus answered them: 'My teaching is not mine, but his who sent me'; if any man's will is to do his will, he shall know whether the teaching is from God or whether I am speaking on my own authority" (Jn. 7, 16-17).

Teaching in the New Testament has an even wider meaning, something which it does not have in the Old; it is a revealing of the deeper background to God's plan of salvation, an explanation of what was already present in the Old Testament — but beyond mankind's understanding.

This and other aspects of "the doctrine" will be discussed more fully further on.

Wisdom

Being the explanation of a doctrine, the preaching of the New Testament in the world of Greek culture of that time came up against the "wisdom" of philosophers and rhetoricians. The Athenian "seekers of wisdom" ask Paul: "May we know what this new teaching is which you present?" (Acts 17, 19). The apostle tells us, in his first letter to the Corinthians, about the conflict between gospel doctrine and Greek philosophy. This gives him a reason for explaining the character of preaching as a wisdom. The preaching offers a wisdom which has nothing in common with purely human wisdom. It can only be considered by the latter as stupidity, for it is "the word of the Cross." But for the believer it is a power for salvation. "For since, in the wisdom of God, the world did not know God through wisdom, it pleased God through the folly of what we preach to save those who believe. For Jews demand signs and Greeks seek wisdom, but we preach Christ crucified, a stumbling block to Jews and folly to Gentiles, but to those who are called, both Jews and Greeks, Christ the power of God and the wisdom of God" (1 Cor. 1, 21-24).

Paul points out to his Christians, however, that the preaching quite definitely offers a wisdom — but only to mature Christians, who are accessible for the deeper workings of God's Spirit: "Yet among the mature we do impart wisdom . . . But we impart a secret and hidden wisdom of God, which God decreed before the ages for our glorification" (1 Cor. 2, 6-7). The wisdom which Paul means, therefore, relates to the timeless plan of God's salvation. It gives the believer a deeper knowledge of this plan of salvation. In last analysis it is nothing else than the Christian **gnosis** (knowledge), which Paul speaks about elsewhere, which is nourished by faith and love — and which leads to the fullness of God (cf. Eph. 3, 17-19).

It is a sign of the great richness and dignity of the preaching, that — as the wisdom of God — it is the source of this knowledge. Here once again we can only fully appreciate the meaning of this New Testament thought against its Old Testament background. The preaching — in as far as it offers wisdom — fulfills the Old Testament ideal of a source of knowledge as a basis for living: "For he who finds me (wisdom) finds life and obtains favor from the Lord" (Prov. 8, 35). This connection with the Old Testament is particularly clear in the gospels. Jesus, speaking about his mission, calls himself "the Wisdom" (Mt. 11, 19; cf. also Mt. 12, 42). Like the Wisdom of the Old Testament, Jesus invites the acceptance of his yoke — his law: "Take my yoke upon you, and learn from me; for I am gentle and lowly in heart" (Mt. 11, 29). In John's gospel, Jesus speaks of himself as the Witness of the Father, whose secrets he knows (cf. Jn. 3, 11-12. 31-32; 8, 26). This calls to mind, once again, Wisdom of whom it is said that she: "Is initiated in the knowledge of God and is his adviser in his works" (Wisd. 8, 4).

Revelation

The above-mentioned text of 1 Cor. 2, 6-7 contains yet another aspect of the preaching — the **revelation** of a secret of God. In the synoptic gospels Jesus refers to the Kingdom of God as a secret, into which the apostles are admitted by his preaching (cf. Mk. 4, 11 etc.). Of himself he says: "All things have been delivered to me by my Father; and no one knows the Son except the Father, and no one knows the Father except the Son and any one to whom the Son chooses to **reveal** him" (Mt. 11, 27). The concept of revelation is inseparable in the Bible from the concepts of secret and "mystery."

In Paul's letters, "secret" or "mystery" is a regularly recurring theme. The content of this is God's

plan of salvation, which includes Jews and Gentiles
and of which Christ is the center. The preachers of
the New Testament have a privilege of being allowed
to proclaim this secret after it has been revealed to
them: "Assuming that you have heard," writes Paul
to the Ephesians, "of the stewardship of God's grace
that was given to me for you, how the mystery was
made known to me by revelation, as I have written
briefly. When you read this you can perceive my
insight into the mystery of Christ, which was not
made known to the sons of men in other generations
as it has now been revealed to his holy apostles and
prophets by the Spirit; that is how the Gentiles are
fellow heirs, members of the same body, and par-
takers of the Promise in Jesus Christ through the
gospel. Of this gospel I was made a minister. . ."
(Eph. 3, 2-7). The apostles are "servants of Christ
and stewards of the mysteries of God" (1 Cor. 4, 1).

This is the highest claim made for the preaching
of the New Testament — it brings revelation of God's
eternal secret, which means salvation for all peoples
(cf. Rom. 16, 25-27).

We first meet the idea of a revelation of God's
secrets — dealing with the future of Israel and of
other peoples — in the book of Daniel (cf. Dan. 2,
18-23; 28-30). It becomes highly developed in the
apocryphal apocalypses ("Revelations") of Judaism
around the time of Christ. In the scrolls of the
Jewish community near the Dead Sea (Qumran)
we also meet the idea, that God gives an insight into
his secrets to certain chosen individuals. When we

find the New Testament seeing preaching as a revelation, then that is its connection with these earlier ideas — to which it gives new meaning.

The picture that emerges from the various terms applied to the preaching by the New Testament is rich and varied. The preaching is the greatest and most overwhelming happening in a new time, a time in which the Old Testament prophecies of salvation are being fulfilled. It is a doctrine giving insight into God's plan of salvation. It is the source of the highest form of wisdom. It leads one into the hidden mysteries of God. Another aspect of preaching appears against the background of the Old Testament; it is something which takes up and renews the content of the forms of God's word in the Old Testament — prophecy, law, wisdom, revelation — fulfilling them in the highest possible sense.

7

THE MESSAGE OF JESUS

After we have seen the fact and the meaning of preaching, our attention is now called to the **content.** In this monograph only the main themes can be dealt with, the themes which we could call the fulcrums, which support the entire framework of the preaching.

Preaching can be described, in a most general sense as God's salvation for mankind. In Acts 13, 26 it is "the message of salvation." If we study the preaching in the New Testament as to its construction, we can distinguish two main parts; we find first of all the proclamation of salvation, with an invitation to accept it — the **message** — which is then followed by a further explanation (i.e. the **doctrine**) for those who have accepted the invitation.

In this and in the following chapter we are dealing with the "message" aspect.

The Kingdom of God

The point of departure for the entire message of salvation in the New Testament is Jesus' preaching. The synoptic gospels give the central theme of his message: the **Kingdom of God.** In biblical language this means first and foremost that God is the **actively ruling Lord,** i.e. "kingdom" is **not** meant in the modern sense. Instead of "Kingdom of God," Matthew uses the expression "Kingdom of heaven"; this is in agreement with Jewish use of language; the latter expression is identical in content to the other and must have come from Jesus himself.

In John the Baptist's preaching we already find the Kingdom of God as a central theme: "In those days came John the Baptist, preaching in the wilderness of Judea: 'Repent, for the kingdom of heaven is at hand'" (Mt. 3, 1-2). Jesus starts his public appearance with it: "After John was arrested, Jesus came into Galilee, preaching the gospel of God, and saying: 'The time is fulfilled, and the Kingdom of God is at hand; repent, and believe in the gospel'" (Mk. 1, 14-15). We find it also in the preaching by Jesus' disciples during his life. Jesus commands them: "Preach as you go, saying: 'the kingdom of heaven is at hand'" (Mt. 10, 7). The evangelists refer to the activities of Jesus and his disciples as "preaching the gospel of the kingdom" or "preaching the kingdom" (cf. Mt. 4, 23; Lk. 4, 43; 9, 2).

The above quoted text from Mark shows how Jesus places his message — about the Kingdom of God — as though all previous history of salvation leads up to it: "The time is fulfilled." The prophecies are being realized. The prophets of the Old Testament expected a coming of God, the King in glory; Israel was to be relieved from exile and suppression: "Sing aloud, O daughter of Zion; shout,

O Israel! Rejoice and exult with all your heart, O
daughter of Jerusalem. The Lord has taken away
the judgments against you, he has cast out your
enemies. The King of Israel, the Lord, is in your
midst; you shall fear evil no more" (Zeph. 3, 14-15).
"How beautiful upon the mountains are the feet of
him who brings good tidings, who publishes peace,
who brings good tidings of good, who publishes
salvation, who says to Zion: 'Your God reigns'" (Is.
52, 7). This definitive and all-embracing kingship
of God means the fullness of salvation for Israel
and for the Gentiles, who will recognize the God
of Israel. As a result of the pressure of Roman
domination, and influenced by apocryphal "scripture," this expectation in the time of Christ had
become very temporal and nationalistic. Jesus turns
his message back toward the authentic prophetical
expectations. In all of his preaching one feels that
he has Daniel's visions particularly in mind. These
portray the dawn of God's reign as an intervention
of heavenly Power in earthly affairs; all that which
opposes God comes to its end and the power is
delegated by God to "the people of the saints of
the Most High" (cf. Dan. 7).

It should be pointed out that Jesus only gradually
reveals the innermost characteristics of the Kingdom
of God. Usually he speaks about them in parables,
which are more an invitation to further thought for
the masses rather than a real revelation. One point,
however, is emphasized from the beginning; Jesus
makes it clear that God's Kingdom terminates the

anti-God power of Satan. Jesus is himself closely involved with this; it is his authoritative command by which evil spirits are cast out. The people are amazed by this: "What is this? A new teaching! With authority he commands even the unclean spirits, and they obey him" (Mk. 1, 27). Jesus himself treats this work of power as a sign of the coming of God's Kingdom: "But if it is by the finger of God that I cast out demons, then the Kingdom of God has come upon you" (Lk. 11, 20). His disciples report to him about their mission: "Lord, even the demons are subject to us in your name! — and he says: "I saw Satan fall like lightning from heaven" (Lk. 10, 17-18). He also gives his preaching and miracles — since they are fulfillments of the prophecies — as a realization of the expected Kingdom. Asked by the Pharisees when the Kingdom of God would be coming, he answers: "The Kingdom of God is not coming with signs to be observed; nor will they say, 'Lo, here it is!' or 'There!' for behold, the Kingdom of God is in the midst of you" (Lk. 17, 20-21). Jesus means that God's Kingdom is there **in his person.**

Let us compare the last three quotations with the earlier cited text of Mk. 1, 14-15; we see how the Kingdom is at once "at hand" and "come upon you." There are other statements which place the coming of the Kingdom in the **future.** At the Last Supper, Jesus says: "From now on I shall not drink the fruit of the vine until the Kingdom of God comes" (Lk. 22, 18). Jesus repeatedly speaks of a future entry into God's Kingdom or an inheritance of it (e.g. Mt.

7, 21; 25, 34). He teaches us to pray: "Thy Kingdom come. . . ." (Mt. 6, 10).

There is in fact no opposition between the "already now" and "not yet" of these texts. The paradox draws our attention to the quite unique and mysterious nature of God's Kingdom as preached by Jesus. It is something that defies human observation and appreciation. It is reality, but as a manifestation of godly power. It **is** already here, in the form of Jesus' words and miracles; but the full revelation has not yet come. We received the kernel of this revelation with the appearance of Jesus; this had to be, because the time is fulfilled. In this sense the Kingdom of God is always at hand. Day and hour of the final completion, however, remain the Father's secret (cf. Mk. 13, 32).

In his gospel John very rarely speaks about the Kingdom of God as subject of Jesus' preaching. He bases and centers everything upon Jesus' **mission.** To this Jesus directs the attention of his audience. For this he asks faith and for this he calls the prophets to witness: "The testimony which I have is greater than that of John; for the works which the Father has granted me to accomplish, these very works which I am doing, bear me witness that the Father has sent me. . . . Do not think that I shall accuse you to the Father; it is Moses who accuses you, on whom you set your hope. If you believed Moses, you would believe me, for he wrote of me. But if you do not believe his writing, how will you believe my words?" (Jn. 5, 36. 45-47). His entire

preaching can be concentrated into this one statement, to the Father: "This is eternal life, that they
know thee the only true God, and Jesus Christ whom
thou hast sent" (Jn. 17, 3).

"Repent and Believe"

Jesus' preaching about the Kingdom of God is accompanied by a call to repentance and belief: "Repent, and believe in the gospel" (Mk. 1, 15). Repentance is also preached by John the Baptist (cf. Mt.
3, 2). The baptism he gives is "a baptism of repentance for the forgiveness of sins" (Mk. 1, 4). On their
missions during Jesus' life, the apostles preached
"that men should repent" (Mk. 6, 12).

Repentance is also a prophetic theme. The
prophets of the Old Testament continually point out
the need for Israel to repent, if it is to be worthy of
its chosen status and is to experience the salvation
of the Lord's rule. "Return faithless Israel, says the
Lord. I will not look on you in anger, for I am
merciful, says the Lord; I will not be angry for
ever. Only acknowledge your guilt" (Jer. 3, 12-13).
The concrete meaning of this repentance is a radical
turnover of a way of life: "Cease to do evil, learn
to do good" (Is. 1, 17). There must be a break with
idolatry, injustice and immorality — the people
must turn and cling to the Lord, in obedience to
his Covenant. The admonitions by John the Baptist
(cf. Lk. 3, 7-14) have similar content.

The call to repentance by John, Jesus and the
apostles, however, implies a different situation to

that of the prophetic call. God's rule is **at hand and is dawning.** Repentance, in their preaching therefore, means above all a state of readiness for this happening. For a sinner this involves a change in his way of life. Even for one who lives justly by human standards there is a change needed. God's rule is a supernatural reality, it is the breakthrough of God's world into earthly relationships. There is a call to every individual to turn his back on his own little world. Repentance means, in the last analysis, the abandonment of human self-sufficiency — the giving over of one's self to God who alone can save. This is the reason why we read that "the Pharisees and the lawyers rejected the purpose of God for themselves" (Lk. 7, 30) when they refused John's baptism.

Repentance is therefore a **decisive moment.** Jesus' preaching presents Israel with a choice — between salvation and ruination. When Jesus is told of the Galileans whom Pilate had killed in the temple, he reacts with: "Do you think that these Galileans were worse sinners than all the other Galileans, because they suffered thus? I tell you, No; but unless you repent you will all likewise perish" (Lk. 13, 1-3).

The requirement of **faith,** together with repentance, calls for a decision also regarding the person of Jesus. One must believe in a gospel — a message of joy — which **he** preaches. The believing of what he preaches is the final step in repentance — the definitive "Yes" to the Kingdom of God. The

evangelist John stresses this requirement of faith
particularly. The concept of repentance does not
occur in his gospel, that of believing does — frequently. John's concept of believing is based on
Jesus as the One Sent by the Father; it is a "coming"
to Jesus in order "that you may have life" (cf. Jn.
5, 40). Belief brings the decision between life and
death: "He who believes in him is not condemned;
he who does not believe is condemned already,
because he has not believed in the name of the only
Son of God" (Jn. 3, 18).

In point of fact, this belief was refused by the
Israel of Jesus' time. It had not understood "the
signs of the times" (cf. Mt. 16, 2-3). It therefore
is excluded — except for a "chosen few" who repent
and believe — from the feast of God's Kingdom (cf.
Mt. 22, 1-10). Jesus concludes one of his parables,
addressed to Israel's leaders, with: "Therefore I tell
you, the Kingdom of God will be taken away from
you and given to a nation producing the fruits of
it" (Mt. 21, 43). This statement became reality after
Jesus' resurrection, when Israel still refused the invitation given by those whom he had sent.

The Son of Man

It is impossible to separate the Kingdom of God
from the person and mission of Jesus Christ. This
becomes completely clear after Jesus' death and
glorification. These throw a light on his mission.
In their turn they are spotlighted by Jesus' preaching
beforehand. The Master himself was the first to

show the connection between God's Kingdom and his own person. He did this particularly by using the Son of Man theme. He used this title for his person by preference — since it expresses all the fundamental aspects of his personality.

Two lines of development converge in the theme of the Son of Man. One of these — dealing with the coming of the Son of Man in glory — starts with the book of Daniel. In chapter 7 we read: "I saw in the night visions, and behold, with the clouds of heaven there came one like a son of man, and he came to the Ancient of Days (God) and was presented before him. And to him was given dominion and glory and kingdom, that all peoples, nations and languages should serve him; his dominion is an everlasting dominion, which shall not pass away, and his kingdom one that shall not be destroyed" (Dan. 7, 13-14). In many of Jesus' statements regarding the Son of Man we hear the echo of this prophecy: "For whoever is ashamed of me and of my words in this adulterous and sinful generation, of him will the Son of Man also be ashamed, when he comes in the glory of his Father with the holy angels" (Mk. 8, 38). "And then they will see the Son of Man coming in clouds with great power and glory" (Mk. 13, 26). "You will see the Son of Man sitting at the right hand of Power, and coming with the clouds of heaven" (Mk. 14, 62). These and similar texts are dealing with the future revelation of the Kingdom of God — and in particular with its completion, its breakthrough, at the end of time.

Jesus, the glorified Son of Man, forms the central point of this.

Jesus also connects the Son of Man title however with another line of development, not one coming from the book of Daniel, but from the prophecies about the suffering Servant of the Lord in the book of Isaiah (cf. Is. 53). We find this line appearing in a number of texts, which deal with the approaching suffering, death and resurrection of the Son of Man. This is the originality of Jesus — that he brings two so widely diverging lines together in the title Son of Man. "He began to teach them that the Son of Man must suffer many things, and be rejected by the elders and the chief priests and the scribes, and be killed, and after three days rise again" (Mk. 8, 31). The regular mention of the resurrection in these texts is another pointer to the glory of the Kingdom of God. It becomes clear, however, that the way to this glory is to be via suffering and death. These have their own purpose; they have the character of a **sacrifice of propitiation** for the sins of humanity: "The Son of Man also came not to be served but to serve, and to give his life as a ransom for many" (Mk. 10, 45). This last is also a key to a striking aspect of Jesus' appearances — his special love for sinners, the appreciation he has of his power on earth to forgive sins (cf. Mk. 2, 10).

The full illumination of the death and glory of the Son of Man, and their connection, is to be found in the Last Supper texts. Jesus speaks at the Last

Supper of his death as being the establishment of a New Covenant through his Blood, which is to be shed for the forgiveness of sins (cf. Mk. 14, 22-24; Lk. 22, 19-22). Besides this he speaks of his entering into the Kingdom of God: "Truly, I say to you, I shall not drink again of the fruit of the vine until that day when I drink it new in the Kingdom of God" (Mk. 14, 25). It follows from the propitiatory and saving nature of his death, that he will not be there alone — but with all those who share in the new Covenant in his Blood. He assures his disciples: "As my Father appointed a Kingdom for me, so do I appoint for you, that you may eat and drink at my table in my Kingdom, and sit on thrones judging the twelve tribes of Israel" (Lk. 22, 29-30).

Suffering and death of the Son of Man are therefore — for himself and for the people of the new Covenant — the way to the glory of the Kingdom of God. This can be put in another way; the departure of the Son of Man — "as it is written of him" (Mk. 14, 21) — is a further approach of the Kingdom. It appears in the dying Jesus as forgiveness of sins; in the risen Christ it is the already present but yet still to be the awaited revelation of God's glorious rule.

8

THE APOSTOLIC KERYGMA

The term **"apostolic kerygma"** refers to the preaching (literally: "proclamation") of salvation by the apostles to the Jewish and Gentile world of their time. In fact, we are thinking of the first preaching to the not-yet-converted, which up to now was referred to as "the message."

We will now review the main themes of the apostolic kerygma in the same way as we did the message of Jesus. The material we need is to be found in the Acts of the Apostles and in their letters. In the Acts, Luke gives a number of characteristic examples of the kerygma — in the form of speeches by the two leading apostles, Peter and Paul. Luke himself may have been responsible for the final form of these statements. On the other hand, the style and content of these speeches — with e.g. their archaic way of expression and Semitic coloration — point to Luke's use of old documentation or tradition as his basis. These quotations therefore provide us with an authentic representation of the apostolic kerygma, in its themes and in its method.

Besides the Acts, the letters of the apostles are a valuable source of information. In contrast to the speeches in the Acts, they are always addressed to already established Christian communities. They assume their readers' knowledge of the kerygma. They either give a deeper explanation of it (i.e. a doctrine regarding God's plan of salvation), or else they deal with the practice of Christian living — but then always linked with kerygma. This means that in the letters we continually meet the great kerygmatic themes; we sometimes find extensive reviews (cf. e.g. chapters 1 and 2 of the first letter of Peter), often there are short formulations — which seem to contain the core of the apostolic message of salvation.

In a moment we shall deal with the elements of the kerygma, one by one. First, however, we give a number of excerpts from the Acts and from the letters, under the heading "Testimony." The idea is to show the various elements of the apostolic message in their mutual connection. As the explanation develops — based on these texts — we will add further material.

Testimony

From the Acts of the Apostles.

Peter is speaking on the day of Pentecost to the people of Jerusalem: "Men of Judea and all who dwell in Jerusalem, let this be known to you, and give ear to my words. For these men are not drunk, as you suppose, since it is only the third hour of the day; but this is what was spoken by the prophet Joel: 'And in the last days it shall be, God declares,

that I will pour out my Spirit upon all flesh, and
your sons and daughters shall prophecy. . . . I will
show wonders in the heaven above and signs on the
earth beneath, blood, and fire, and vapor of smoke;
the sun shall be turned into darkness and the moon
into blood, before the Day of the Lord comes, the
great and manifest day. And it shall be that whoever
calls on the Name of the Lord shall be saved.' Men
of Israel, hear these words: Jesus of Nazareth, a
man attested to you by God with mighty works and
wonders and signs which God did through him in
your midst, as you yourselves know — this Jesus,
delivered up according to the definitive plan and
foreknowledge of God, you crucified and killed by
the hands of lawless men. But God raised him up,
having loosed the pangs of death, because it was
not possible for him to be held by it." Peter then
points out how Jesus fulfills — in his resurrection
— David's prophecy, and continues: "This Jesus
God raised up, and of that we are all witnesses.
Being therefore exalted at the right hand of God,
and having received from the Father the promise
of the Holy Spirit, he has poured out this which
you see and hear. . . Let all the house of Israel
therefore know assuredly that God has made him
both Lord and Christ, this Jesus who you crucified."
When the people ask the apostles what they have
to do, Peter answers: "Repent, and be baptized every
one of you in the name of Jesus Christ for the forgiveness of your sins; and you shall receive the gift
of the Holy Spirit. For the promise is to you and to
your children and to all that are far off, every one

whom the Lord our God calls to him" (Acts 2, 14-39).

After the curing of the lame man in the temple at Jerusalem, Peter with John beside him once again declares witness of Jesus' resurrection: "But God raised him from the dead. To this we are witnesses. And his name, by faith in his name, has made this man strong whom you see and know; and the faith which is through him has given the man this perfect health in the presence of you all. And now, brethren, I know that you acted in ignorance, as did also your rulers. But what God foretold by the mouth of all the prophets, that his Christ should suffer, he thus fulfilled. Repent therefore, and turn again, that your sins may be blotted out. . ." (Acts 3, 15-19). The next day Peter is before the High Council. When it demands an explanation of his conduct, he declares: "He (Jesus) is 'the stone which was rejected by you builders, but which has become the head of the corner.' And there is salvation in no one else, for there is no other name under heaven given among men by which we must be saved" (Acts 4, 11-12).

Very interesting in its content and formulation is the first kerygma to a pagan audience; Luke is describing Peter's visit to the centurion Cornelius: "Peter opened his mouth and said. . . . This is the word which he sent to Israel, preaching good news of peace by Jesus Christ — he is Lord of all. You know the word which was proclaimed throughout all Judea, beginning from Galilee after the baptism which John preached: how God anointed Jesus of

Nazareth with the Holy Spirit and with power; how he went about doing good and healing all that were oppressed by the devil, for God was with him. And we are witnesses to all that he did both in the country of the Jews and in Jerusalem. They put him to death by hanging him on a tree; but God raised him on the third day and made him manifest; not to all the people but to us who were chosen by God as witnesses, who ate and drank with him after he rose from the dead. And he commanded us to preach to the people, and to testify that he is the one ordained by God to be judge of the living and the dead. To him all the prophets bear witness that every one who believes in him receives forgiveness of sins through his name" (Acts 10, 34-43).

Of entirely different conception is the speech given by Paul to another pagan audience, in the Areopagus at Athens: "Men of Athens, I perceive that in every way you are very religious. For as I passed along, and observed the objects of your worship, I found also an altar with this inscription, 'To an unknown God.' What therefore you worship as unknown, this I proclaim to you. The God who made the world and everything in it, being Lord of heaven and earth, does not live in shrines made by man, nor is he served by human hands, as though he needed anything, since he himself gives to all men life and breath and everything. And he made from one every nation of men to live on all the face of the earth, having determined allotted periods and the boundaries of their inhabitation, that they should seek God, in the hope that they might feel after him and find him — for he is not far from each one of us." He points out the undignified nature of idolatry, and continues: "The times of ignorance God overlooked, but now he commands all men everywhere to repent; because he has fixed a day on which he will judge the world in righteousness by a man whom he has appointed, and of this he has given assurance to all men by raising him from the dead" (Acts 17, 22-31).

From the apostolic letters we have selected a few of the more important resumés of the kerygma. They are all drawn from Paul's letters, and they deal in chronological order with the greater part of his apostolic career.

In his first letter to the Thessalonians, Paul reviews the results of his preaching to them: ". . . how you turned to God from idols, to serve a living and true God, and to wait for his Son from heaven, whom he raised from the dead, Jesus who delivers us from the wrath to come" (1 Thess. 1, 9-10). It is clear that Paul is reminding the people of Thessalonica of the main themes of his preaching to them.

At the beginning of his letter to the Galatians, he writes: "Grace to you and peace from God the Father and our Lord Jesus Christ, who gave himself for our sins to deliver us from the present evil age, according to the will of our God and Father" (Gal. 1, 3-4).

The text of 1 Cor. 15, 1-8. — which refers to the

earliest origins of the kerygma — was already par-
tially quoted on p. 37. The second part sums up
the appearance of the risen Christ to the apostles
and disciples.

Paul gives a masterly explanation of the content
of the Gospel in his letter to the Romans. He opens
with a note on the origins and central theme of
the Gospel: "Paul, a servant of Jesus Christ, called
to be an apostle, set apart for the gospel of God
which he promised beforehand through his prophets
in the holy Scriptures, the gospel concerning his
Son, who was descended from David according to
the flesh and designated Son of God in power according to the Spirit of Holiness by his resurrection
from the dead, Jesus Christ our Lord; through whom
we have received grace and apostleship to bring
about the obedience of faith for the sake of his name,
among all nations" (Rom. 1, 1-5).

Faith is for us — as it was for Abraham — the
way to justification: "It will be reckoned to us who
believe in him that raised from the dead Jesus our
Lord, who was put to death for our trespasses and
raised for our justification" (Rom. 4, 24-25).

"If you confess with your lips that Jesus is Lord
and believe in your heart that God raised him from
the dead, you will be saved" (Rom. 10, 9).

The imprisoned Paul works out in great detail the
content of the "mystery of salvation." He sums it
up, in the letter to the Colossians, as: "Christ in
you, the hope of glory" (Col. 1, 27).

A testimony, dating from the last phase of Paul's apostolate: "But when the goodness and loving kindness of God our Savior appeared, he saved us, not because of deeds done by us in righteousness, but in virtue of his own mercy, by the washing of regeneration and renewal in the Holy Spirit, which he poured out upon us richly through Jesus Christ our Savior, so that we might be justified by his grace and become heirs in hope of eternal life" (Tit. 3, 4-7).

The Message of Salvation

The most general aspect of the kerygma — its whole aim in fact — is **salvation.** Paul speaks about the preaching as "the message of this salvation" (Acts 13, 26), or "this salvation of God" (Acts 28, 28). Elsewhere we find "the words of this Life" (Acts 5, 20). The salvation motif is present in all the selected extracts, either specifically mentioned or at least in the background. It is fundamental to the whole of the New Testament preaching. "Save yourselves from this corrupt generation" is Peter's exhortation at Pentecost (Acts 2, 40). The members of the Christian community are referred to as "those who are being saved" (Acts 2, 47).

The salvation of the New Testament is no state of general happines or blessedness — it is quite definitely a **saving** from threatening peril. Paul contrasts those "who are being saved" with those "who are perishing" (1 Cor. 1, 18; 2 Cor. 2, 15). Salvation means that "Jesus . . . delivers us from the wrath to come" (1 Thess. 1, 10). We are to be saved from the peril with which God's wrath confronts mankind, the complete and final destruction. The contrast between salvation and destruction in the New Testament is also formulated as a contrast between life and death, particularly by Paul and John. The giver of life, of salvation, is God and is Jesus Christ the "Savior."

We see that the message of salvation places mankind before an all-encompassing and definitive **decision.** This is accentuated in the preaching, at the conclusion of the message, by a reference to the coming judgment (cf. Acts 10 and 17, excerpts above) — which awaits the "scoffers" who "do not listen" (cf. Acts 13, 40-41 resp. 3, 23). The necessity of a choice splits the hearers of the preaching into two camps — which as it were confront each other with the opponents of the preaching as a rule persecuting those who believe. One reads many examples of this in the Acts.

The above excerpts also give an impression of the method of the kerygma, particularly as regards its point of departure. In some cases — such as the Pentecost statement, after the curing of the lame man and in the Areopagus — this is a concrete datum or occurence. As a general rule the kerygma connects up with the longing for salvation, which was particularly strong at that time both in Israel and in the pagan world. In Israel there was the expectation of the promise (cf. Acts 2, 39), the blessing promised to Abraham (cf. Acts 3, 25-26), the "refreshment" (cf. Acts 3, 19) and — in the circles of the really devout — the need for forgiveness of sins which was beyond the power of the Mosaic law (cf. Acts 13, 38-39; 15, 10). In the pagan world there was a kind of vague religious feeling — "what therefore you worship as unknown. . . ." (Acts 17, 23) — a search for salvation, redemption, immortality, as we meet this in the mystery religions. The impression could be gained from Acts 16, 17 that the preaching to the pagans did make contact with such a search; Paul and his helpers are described — in a pagan surrounding — as men who were proclaiming the way of salvation. The framework of the letter to the Romans suggests that moral hopelessness — of both Jews and pagans — played a part at the introduction of the actual message of salvation itself (cf. Rom. 1-3). For the slaves and common people of the civilization of the time the sheer misery of existence in general may have served as the connecting-point.

Jesus, the Lord and the Christ

The very heart of the kerygma is Jesus as the Lord and the Christ. His person typifies the entire content of the preaching. There is the telling of the "good news of Jesus" (Acts 8, 35), the "proclamation" of "the Christ" (Acts 8, 5), the "preaching" of "the Lord Jesus" (Acts 11, 20) and the "teaching and preaching" of "Jesus as the Christ" (Acts 5, 42). The expressions "the word of the Lord" (Acts 15, 35-36) and "the gospel of Jesus Christ, the Son of God" (Mk. 1, 1) make it quite clear that Jesus the Lord is origin and center of the kerygma.

The speeches in the Acts give the general trend of the kerygma regarding Jesus. After short mention of his public life in Israel, with an occasional reference to his descent from the house of David (cf. Acts 2, 30; 13, 23; Rom. 1, 3), a description is given of his death at the hands of the Jews. Then comes the climax with the witness to his resurrection, frequently followed by a statement about his glorification or exaltation by God (cf. also Acts 3, 13; 5, 31). Jesus' resurrection is always described as being the work of God, who "raised him up." Resurrection and exaltation make Jesus "Lord and Christ" (Acts 2, 36); they give him — also as man — the full possession of the godly glory and ruling power; they form the solemn publication of his dignity as Christ — "the Anointed One" — the Messiah-King who leads both Jews and Gentiles to salvation. The formulation of Rom. 1, 4 — Jesus is designated by his resurrection as "Son of God in power" — comes very close to that of Acts 2, 36.

In the speeches reported in the Acts we can trace a certain line of development, which is terminated in the apostolic letters. We find that certain points of the kerygma — present in it from the beginning, but not at first clearly propounded — are gradually brought more and more sharply into the foreground. From the start the kerygma preaches the godly glory of Jesus as **Kyrios** (Lord), which implies the godly character of his person; but Paul is the first to use the specific title "Son of God" for Jesus (cf. Acts 9, 20; 13, 33) — and he does this regularly in his letters. Another point which is not at first directly stated is the sacrificial nature of Jesus' death. It is given with references to God's plan (cf. Acts 2, 23; 4, 27-28) and also to the prophecies (cf. Acts 3, 18; 13, 27-29), particularly those regarding the Servant of God (Acts 3, 13-14; 8, 32-35). Otherwise the forgiveness of sins is treated more directly as the **glorified** Christ's work of salvation (cf. Acts 2, 38; 5, 31). Paul speaks however, in his first letter, specifically of the **death** of Jesus "for us" (1 Thess. 5, 10) and later of his dying "for our sins" (see excerpts). We find a certain development also in the expectations regarding the end of time. Peter's speech at Pentecost expresses these in the words of the prophet Joel as the coming of "the Day of the Lord" (Acts 2, 20); the Acts 3 speech refers to the "sending" of Jesus when "all the families of the earth" shall "be blessed." The kerygma speaks to the pagans of Jesus future appearance as the Judge of the living and the dead (Acts 10, 42; 17, 31). Paul's speech to the Jews of Antioch in Asia-Minor also hints at a future judgment (Acts 13, 40-41). In the early letters by Paul we find a Greek term, which becomes the normal one in the New Testament: **parousia** — meaning "a coming" (with particular reference to the Lord's coming). The earliest text in this connection, 1 Thess. 9-10, places the expectation of this coming centrally — and this is in fact characteristic of the two letters to the Thessalonians. The context shows that expectation of the Lord's coming is closely related to belief in the resurrection and is indeed derived immediately from it. This expectation is not everywhere so strikingly put as in Paul's first two letters; but it is continually being made clear that expectation of the Lord's coming again, along with his death and resurrection, forms one of the essential elements of the kerygma. A text as, for instance, Col. 1, 27 expresses the same expectation in a somewhat different form with the phrase "Christ in you, the hope of glory" (cf. also Tit. 3, 7).

We can therefore say that a certain development of the kerygma about Jesus takes place, starting from a core which already contains all the essential elements — just like the unfolding of a leaf and a flower from the bud. Gripped by the overwhelming event of Jesus' resurrection, the apostles preached this as the start of a new age — with the risen and glorified Christ himself as the source of salvation for all believers. The immediate background was formed by the expectation of a final completion of this salvation by the same Christ, giving a new concrete expression to the expectation of the Kingdom of God and of the "Day," which were both inherited from the Old Testament and from Jesus himself. Reflecting on Jesus' death in the light of the prophecies — and also in connection with his own words — the preaching gave a gradually sharpening outline to its sacrificial character and propitiating power.

The most important aspect of all of this — with an eye to the correct insight into the preaching of the New Testament — **is that the death and resurrection of Jesus are from the very beginning inseparably interconnected in the kerygma.** They are the two aspects of **one** salvatory happening, continually calling each other to mind. The above quoted text of Rom. 4, 25 (excerpts) is important in this connection.

The excerpts also show us that the kerygma made mention from the start of the Lord's descent from the house of David, of his life on earth and of the circumstances of his death and burial. It is only to be expected that this would be done more thoroughly for the non-Jews and for the Jews outside Palestine than for the people of Jerusalem and Palestine (compare the speech of Acts 2 with those of Acts 10 and 13). However, a more detailed explanation of all these matters did not belong to the kerygma but to the doctrine.

The Fulfillment of the Prophecies

A recurring tendency of the kerygma is to portray the death and resurrection of Jesus — and its working toward salvation — as the fulfillment of the prophecies. This is done sometimes in general terms (cf. Acts 10, 43; Rom. 1, 2), but usually there is a reference to a certain text or texts. The resurrection of Christ is seen particularly as the fulfillment of a number of Psalm-sayings by David, who "was a prophet" (Acts 2, 30); the Psalms in question are Ps. 2, 16, 110, 132 (cf. e.g. Acts 2). Before Jesus' death there is a preference for the prophecies about the Servant of God in the book of Isaiah (particularly chapter 53) — (cf. Acts 3, 13-14. 26; 8, 32-35). Also applied to Jesus and his mission are texts from the

Pentateuch or law of Moses, such as Gen. 12, 3; Deut. 18, 15 (cf. Acts 3, 22-26). This usage of Old Testament texts with regard to Jesus is in accordance with what he himself said: "Everything written about me in the law of Moses and the prophets and the psalms must be fulfilled" (Lk. 24, 44).

This latest text — and also others such as Acts 3, 18; Rom. 1, 2 — show us that the calling upon prophetic witness is not in last analysis the collection of some loose texts. No, there is a conviction that **all** prophets — therefore the **entire** expectation of salvation in the Old Testament — have received their fulfillment in Jesus. Now, the central theme in prophetic expectation of salvation is that of the coming of God's Kingdom, the day on which a mighty action of God will destroy the anti-God powers and replace the existing order of things with a new. There will be a complete change, a re-creation of Israel and humanity: "For behold, I create new heavens and a new earth; and the former things shall not be remembered or come into mind. But be glad and rejoice for ever in that which I create; for behold, I create Jerusalem a rejoicing, and her people a joy" (Is. 65, 17-18).

When the kerygma declares that "all the prophets who have spoken . . also proclaimed these days" (Acts 3, 24), then it means nothing less than this: Jesus' death and resurrection are the signs of a mighty and decisive action by God, by which a new order of things is established, a new age, a new people of God, a new humanity, a new creation.

The risen Lord is himself the first among this new people of God and this new humanity, "the first to rise from the dead" (Acts 26, 23). This is the point of expressions such as "a new creation" (2 Cor. 5, 17), "the new nature" (Col. 3, 10), "the age to come" (Hebr. 6, 5) — which are contrasted with "the old," "the old nature" (i.e. of man), "the evil age" (Gal. 1, 4). Along the same line are to be placed such concepts as "the end of time" (1 Pet. 1, 20), "washing of regeneration and renewal" (Tit. 3, 5), "day of redemption" (Eph. 4, 30), "condemnation of sin" (Rom. 8, 3), "triumph over the principalities and powers" (Col. 2, 15), abolition of the "law of commandments and ordinances" (i.e. of Moses) (Eph. 2, 15). All these concepts illustrate the unique nature and import of Christ's work of salvation.

The most remarkable instance of an understanding of the total renewal which Jesus' resurrection brings is the belief in the future **resurrection of the dead.** This theme occurs already in the Acts, where Luke's formulation shows that it flows forth directly from belief in the resurrection of Jesus. The apostles "proclaimed in Jesus the resurrection from the dead" (Acts 4, 2). At Athens, Paul preaches the gospel of "Jesus and the resurrection" (Acts 17, 18). In his conflict with Judaism, Paul identifies the resurrection of the dead with the content of his preaching: "With respect to the hope of the resurrection of the dead I am on trial" (Acts 23, 6). He calls it the promise "to which our twelve tribes hope to attain" made by God to "our fathers" (Acts 26, 6-8). The actual place of the resurrection of the dead in the kerygma appears later, particularly in the first letter to the Corinthians. Paul works it out thoroughly for the sceptical Greeks, once again starting with Christ's resurrection (chap. 15).

The fulfillment of the prophecies is of such fundamental importance that it is understandable that we find a reference to it in the kerygma for pagans (cf. Acts 10, 43). This reference was doubtless fairly general in its terms. In the kerygma for Jews the reference was anything but general, as we can see from Acts 2.3 and 13. At other points in the Acts we also find such references, in particular those dealing with Paul's ministry: "Paul went in, as was his custom, and for three sabbaths he argued with them (the Jews in the synagogue at Thessalonica) from the Scriptures. He explained and proved that it was necessary for the Christ to suffer and to rise from the dead, saying: 'This Jesus, whom I proclaim to you, is the Christ' " (Acts 17, 2-3). It is an "examination of the Scriptures" with his Jewish hearers (Acts 17, 11; cf. also Acts 18, 4; 19, 8; 28, 23).

The introduction to the actual kerygma itself contains, besides a reference to the prophets, a review of the preceding history of Israel's salvation (cf. Acts 13, 17-23). The equivalent of this in pagan surroundings is a review of the history of humanity, as given by Paul in his speech in the Areopagus (Acts 17). The intention behind this procedure is to show the **continuity,** the progressing line, of God's actions.

The new happenings, Jesus' death and resurrection, do not place before Israel and the rest of humanity the problem of making a break with the past. On the contrary, they connect with that past; they are of a different order, but "incarnate" in the world's existence. They are the completion of Israel's election, the highest realization of God's "love for man" (cf. Tit. 3, 4) which was operative in Israel and among the other peoples since the very beginning.

Forgiveness of Sins and the Gift of the Spirit

The immediate effects of Jesus' resurrection and glorification are the forgiving of sins and the giving of the Holy Spirit. In the Acts these are regularly specified as forming the risen and glorified Christ's work of salvation: "God exalted him (Jesus) at his right hand as Leader and Savior, to give repentance to Israel and forgiveness of sins. And we are witnesses to these things, and so is the Holy Spirit whom God has given to those who obey him" (Acts 5, 31-32; cf. also 2, 38; 10, 43). In the prophetic literature of the Old Testament the forgiveness of sins and the gift of the Spirit are the greatest goods of salvation in the messianic age (cf. Hos. 14; Jer. 31, 34; 36, 24-27; Joel 3, 1-4). Between these two there is an intimate connection: the renewing of the heart — which sets the seal on the forgiveness of sin — is an operation by the Spirit of God (cf. Ps. 51, 12-13 and Ezek.).

The element of forgiveness of sins remains characteristic for the kerygma of the entire New Testament, although the formulation often differs from that in the Acts. There is mention of the death of Jesus for our sins, of Jesus as expiation offering (1 Jn. 2, 2), of justification (letter to the Romans), redemption (Eph. 1, 7), cleansing (1 Jn. 1, 7). Paul describes the preaching as "the ministry of reconciliation" (2 Cor. 5, 18-19).

Just as in the Old Testament, there is in the apostolic kerygma also a close connection between forgiveness of sins and gift of the Spirit. According to the text from Joel with which Peter explains the Pentecost miracle, the pouring out of the Holy Spirit reaches its completion with the redemption of mankind (cf. Acts 2, 17-21). The coming down of the Spirit upon pagans even before their baptism (cf. Acts 10, 44-48) means that their "hearts are cleansed by faith" (Acts 15, 9). In the text of Tit. 3, 4-7 we find redemption, renewal, justification and eternal life mentioned as being given to us by God with the pouring out of his Spirit.

As an externally perceptible happening the descent of the Holy Spirit is a sign — of Jesus' glorification (Acts 2, 33) and of the arrival of the "last days," the announcement of the Day of the Lord (Acts 2, 17-21). The Holy Spirit is the Promise (Acts 2, 33), the real fulfillment of the messianic expectations for the people of God and the termination of Jesus' work of salvation (cf. also Acts 1, 5. 8). The descent or impartation of the Holy Spirit therefore always forms a high point in the account of the Acts (cf. 2; 8, 14-19; 10, 44-48; 19, 1-6). It is the end-point of

the kerygma, the actual realization of the messianic
salvation. Whenever the impartation takes place with
an external rite, then this is the "laying on of hands"
by the apostles.

The Holy Spirit theme recurs in all kinds of varia-
tions in the apostolic letters (cf. the text of Tit. 3,
4-7). We meet it in texts which echo old kerygmatic
formulations: "God, who gives his Holy Spirit to
you" (1 Thess. 4, 8). "For through the Spirit, by
faith, we wait for the hope of righteousness" (Gal.
5, 5). It is remarkable that in one of the latest writings of the New Testament there is mention of the
Holy Spirit as the **lasting** source of forgiveness for
sins in the Church: "Receive the Holy Spirit. If
you forgive the sins of any, they are forgiven: if
you retain the sins of any, they are retained" (Jn.
20, 22-23).

Repentance and Belief

God's salvation faces mankind with a choice. The
essence of the kerygma therefore includes a clear
requirement for mankind, which points the way to
salvation at the same time. In our selected excerpts
— and in many other texts from the Acts — we find
that the requirement is **repent** and **believe.** Jesus'
message already contained this double requirement
(cf. Mk. 1, 15). Repentance involves a turning (to
the New) and we find the actual joining of the
Christian community described as a "turning to the
Lord" (cf. Acts 9, 35; 11, 21), or as "believing" (Acts
4, 4; 18, 8). The Christians are "those who believed"

(Acts 2, 44; 4, 32). Repentance and belief are sealed
in baptism, which gives forgiveness of sins (Acts 2,
38; 18, 8). This last is sometimes described as the
fruit of repentance and of belief itself. The Lord
says to Paul: "I have delivered you from the people
and from the Gentiles — to whom I send you to
open their eyes, that they may turn from darkness
to light and from the power of Satan to God, that
they may receive forgiveness of sins and a place
among those who are sanctified by faith in me"
(Acts 26, 17-18).

Repentance and belief are themselves a gift of
God: "To the Gentiles also God has granted repentance unto life" (Acts 11, 18). "As many as were
ordained to eternal life believed" (Acts 13, 48; cf.
also Acts 5, 31; 14, 27).

The meaning of repentance was explained in an
earlier chapter (cf. p. 65). Alongside the more usual
term — which means "changing of attitude" (and of
life) — we find Luke particularly using the verb
"to turn" (see above). The repentance is as a rule
toward God. For pagans it is in fact a turning from
idols to "the living God" (cf. Acts 14, 15; 1 Thess. 1,
9). The belief is usually in Jesus, the Lord. Paul
"testified both to Jews and to Greeks of repentance
to God and of faith in our Lord Jesus Christ" (Acts
20, 21). We do find repentance "to the Lord,"
however, as well as belief "in God" (cf. Acts 16, 34 —
in this case re. pagans).

In the apostolic letters, particularly in those by
Paul, and in John's writing we find the idea of

repentance very much in the background. The way to salvation is mainly identified with **belief,** and this includes the entire process of growth towards becoming a Christian. The steps by which the faith is received are: hearing — attentive listening — acceptance, allowing one's self to be convinced — belief (cf. Acts 8, 6; 16, 14; 17, 4; 28, 28). The process is often shortened to: hearing — belief: "Many of those who heard the word believed" (Acts 4, 4). Clearly there can be **no faith without preaching:** "How are men to call upon him (Christ) in whom they have not believed? And how are they to believe in him of whom they have never heard? And how are they to hear without a preacher?" (Rom. 10, 14-15). In the same way as the preaching is "the word of faith" (Rom. 10, 8), it is also "the word . . . which you heard" (1 Thess. 2, 13) i.e. it is meant to be heeded. Now, in the same way as the preaching comes to the individual as an audible word, his faith must be expressed as an audible answer — the **confession;** at this point the believer first becomes a member of the Christian **community.**

The final aim of faith is salvation: "Without having seen him (Jesus Christ) you love him; though you do not now see him you believe in him and rejoice with unutterable and exalted joy. As the outcome of your faith you obtain the salvation of your souls" (1 Pet. 1, 8-9).

The content of the apostolic kerygma can therefore be condensed to **the fact of Jesus.** It is the message of the dead and glorified Lord Jesus Christ as the only source of salvation for Jews and Gentiles. It is therefore an invitation to salvation, but at the same time a call to repentance and belief. It is set in a perspective of the coming-in-glory of the Lord Jesus, who will be judge of the living and the dead — but who is also the one who brings completed salvation to those who have believed. It would be difficult to find a more concise and terse expression of all this than the kerygmatic formulation of the letter to the Romans: "If you confess with your lips that Jesus is Lord and believe in your heart that God raised him from the dead, you will be saved" (Rom. 10, 9).

When it is stated that the preachers proclaim "the word" (Acts 8, 4; 11, 19), or that they are the "ministers of the word" (Lk. 1, 2), then the very term calls the fact of Jesus to mind. How close together word and fact lie is proved by the connection in Acts 10, 36-38, where the word sent by God turns out to be Jesus of Nazareth. From here to "the Word" — as John preaches in the prologue of his gospel — is but a single step.

We have found a movement — within the apostolic kerygma — of the central theme of the preaching. In the place of the Kingdom of God — which dominated Jesus' message — this theme becomes the fact of Jesus. Yet, the Kingdom of God continues to form the background of the apostolic preaching. The motif returns regularly. "God, who calls you into his own Kingdom and glory," writes Paul in his very first letter (1 Thess. 2, 12). Elsewhere: "Those who do such things shall not inherit the Kingdom of God" (Gal. 5, 21). But the concept "Kingdom of God" now takes turns with "Kingdom of the Son, of Jesus Christ" (cf. e.g. Col. 1, 13).

Since apostolic times God's Kingdom and the fact of Jesus are the two poles of the message of salvation. The two themes are closely associated with each other, but each has its own graduation. Luke makes this clear in the Acts. While he describes Paul, elsewhere in the Acts, as speaking about the Kingdom of God (Acts 19, 8) or proclaiming God's Kingdom (Acts 20, 25), he concludes his book with the following carefully chosen formulation: "He (Paul) preached the Kingdom of God, and taught about the Lord Jesus Christ quite openly and unhindered" (Acts 28, 31; cf. also Acts 8, 12; 28, 23).

Jesus' death and glorification are a first realization of God's Kingdom. Moreover they open up a vista on the full revelation of this Kingdom — the obtaining of "the glory of Our Lord Jesus Christ," which is the glory of "God our Father, who loved us" (2 Thess. 2, 14-16).

9

THE DOCTRINE

We have already pointed out that the "doctrine," the teaching, is a very important part of the New Testament preaching, taking its place beside the kerygma. This chapter first deals generally with the relationship between doctrine and kerygma, following this with further explanations of a few aspects of the doctrine from the standpoint of this relationship in particular. Besides the normal Greek term for "learning" and "doctrine" — which we find, for example, in the name of an early Christian work (first century A.D.), the **Didachè** — the New Testament also uses the related substantive noun **didascalia** (particularly in the letters to Timothy and Titus), as well as a verb from which our word "catechism" is derived.

Around the kerygma

There is a close connection between the kerygma and the doctrine. It is said that Jesus and the apostles preached the gospel (the "good news"), proclaimed salvation **and** taught (cf. pp. 52-54). The texts give us this impression: kerygma and doctrine belong together, with doctrine as a supplement to and continuation of the kerygma. This is clearly the case in Acts 2, 42: those who were baptized at Pentecost "devoted themselves to the apostles' teaching and fellowship, to the breaking of bread and the prayers." We find baptism here between kerygma and doctrine. This can be explained from the rather special situation not only of the day of Pentecost, but also of the hearers — who knew already to some extent Jesus' person and doctrine. Elsewhere the kerygma merges naturally with the doctrine — regarding Jesus, his life, his mission and his law — forming as it were an alloy with it. The baptism then occurred as the termination of a certain phase of the teaching. This is the sense in which we must interpret the statements about the apostles at Jerusalem, Antioch, Ephesus, Rome, "teaching and preaching Jesus as the Christ" (Acts 5, 42; 15, 35; 20, 20-21; 28, 31; the verb "teach" twice comes first). The same applies to Paul's year-and-a-half at Corinth, "teaching the word of God" (Acts 18, 11).

In Jesus public appearances we already find message and doctrine flowing into each other: "He (Jesus) went about all Galilee, teaching in their synagogues and preaching the Gospel of the Kingdom" (Mt. 4, 23). One of the great moments of Jesus' life — the so called "day of parables" — is introduced by Mark, with emphasis on the teaching aspect: "Again he began to teach beside the sea. And a very large crowd gathered about him . . . And he taught them many things in parables, and in his teaching he said to them . . ." (Mk. 4, 1-2). Throughout this chapter — and also in the parallel chapters of Matthew and Luke — we see one of the characteristic aspects of Jesus' teaching in operation. He speaks about the Kingdom of God in parables "as far as they were able to understand it" (Mk. 4, 33); he gives a further explanation of the message of salvation in a way matched to the people's ability to absorb it. In a similar way Jesus arranged his teaching of the apostles later on: "They went on from there and passed through Galilee. And he would not have any one know it; for he was teaching his disciples" (Mk. 9, 30-31). This teaching of his disciples dealt in fact with the supreme matter of his suffering, death and resurrection.

We can conclude from all this what is meant by the most general sense of the teaching: **a broader and deeper development of the message, the kerygma.** This is also expressed in what Paul writes to the Ephesians: "That is not how you were taught about Christ." You have heard about him (kerygma) and were taught in him (doctrine) what the truth is in Jesus" (Eph. 4, 20-21). Kerygma and doctrine are as such separate entities; the latter is a further development of the former. Yet they are one in their subject — both of them center upon Christ. It is just this unity which permits the first letter to Timothy to speak of the entire Christian confession of faith as "the Teaching": "Let all who are under the yoke of slavery regard their masters as worthy of all honor, so that the name of God and the teaching may not be defamed" (1 Tim. 6, 1).

As one might expect, a major role in the doctrine

is played by references to Scripture — just as in
the kerygma. Indeed the calling upon Scripture in
the kerygma is really already the beginning of
doctrine. A typical example of the function of Old
Testament Scripture in Jesus' own teaching is given
by the episode in the synagogue at Nazareth (Lk.
4, 16-21). Peter's first letter is particularly illumin-
ating with regard to the apostolic preaching. The
first part of this letter (1, 3 — 2, 10) is a summary of
what could be called "baptism catechism." In spite
of the fact that this letter is addressed to Gentile
Christians the catechism is full of biblical texts and
reminiscences. In this continual pointing back to the
Old Testament we discover the deepest meaning of
the teaching in the apostolic preaching. With the
aid of Scripture and the history of salvation in the
Old Testament it wishes to give insight into the
economy of salvation, i.e. God's way with Israel
and mankind in general; it wishes to reveal the
deeper background to God's plan and will of salvation.

Naturally, teaching remained an indispensible element for those who were baptized. It became the
task of teachers, who are mentioned as forming a
separate category in the Christian communities (cf.
Acts 13, 1; Rom. 12, 7; Eph. 4, 11). In the letters to
Timothy and Titus the doctrine (**didascalia**) is given
as their foremost task, as it is for the bishops (the
word means "supervisors") and the elders who are
the leaders of the individual churches: "Till I come,
attend to the public reading of Scripture, to preach-

ing, to teaching. . . . Take heed to yourself and to your teaching; hold to that, for by so doing you will save both yourself and your hearers" (1 Tim. 4, 13-16). "Let the elders who rule well be considered worthy of double honor, especially those who labor in preaching and teaching" (1 Tim. 5, 17; cf. also Tit. 1, 9). In the letter to the Galatians we meet the catechist: "Let him who is taught the word (i.e. the catechumen) share all good things with him (the catechist) who teaches" (Gal. 6, 6).

The apostolic letters are in fact largely concerned with further explanation or renewed urging of the teaching, both that regarding the faith and that dealing with the way of life. As instances of the former we mention the treatments of the "coming again" (the letters to the Thessalonians), the justification by faith and the richness of Christ's work of salvation (Rom. 1-8), the resurrection of the dead (1 Cor. 15), the mystery of the Church (Eph. 1-3), Jesus as High Priest of the New Covenant (letter to the Hebrews). In the letters we find that the preceding teaching is always assumed and often referred to: "Do you not remember that when I was still with you I told you this?" (2 Thess. 2, 5). The actual kerygma is also continuously present, in the background, as we see from the regularly returning kerygmatic formulations.

Finally we find the inclusion of what Paul calls "wisdom" (cf. p. 55) in the preaching for the confirmed Christians. This wisdom is also a continuation from the kerygma, forming the ideal conclusion of the preaching and representing desirable perfection to all Christians. Paul makes this clear in his letter to the church of Colossae. After summing up the kerygma's content as "Christ in you, the hope of glory," he goes on: "Him we proclaim, warning every man and teaching every man in all wisdom, that we may present every man mature in Christ. For this I toil, striving with all the energy which he mightily inspires within me" (Col. 1, 27-29).

"What Jesus did and taught . . ."

In the prologue to the Acts of the apostles Luke describes his first book — his gospel — as containing "All that Jesus began to do and teach, until the day when he was taken up, after he had given commandment through the Holy Spirit to the apostles whom he had chosen" (Acts 1, 1-2). The very existence of the four gospels, all dealing with "the doings and teachings" of Jesus during his earthly life and with the appearances of the Risen One, shows that all of this formed a very prominent part of the doctrine. Luke, on the other hand, gives the specific purpose of his gospel: "that you may know the truth concerning the things (doctrine) of which you have been informed (one could translate this with: . . . in which you have received catechism)" (Lk. 1, 4).

An extensive discussion of the gospels is not in order here. We wish only to trace their general outlines as elements of the doctrine and their relationship of the kerygma.

From the very start we find information in the kerygma regarding Jesus' descent from David, his earthly life, the end of this life and his appearances after his resurrection (cf. the speeches from the Acts, pp. 8, 1-3, and Acts 13, 24-31; Rom. 1, 3; 1 Cor. 15, 5-8). These texts show clear appreciation of the fact that the risen and glorified Christ is none other than Jesus of Nazareth. The important thing is not only this identity as such, however, but also the **meaning** of all this information. Jesus' descent from David belongs to his nature as Messiah; his miracles — worked by the power of the Holy Spirit — prove that the prophecies about the time of salvation are fulfilled in him. The circumstances of his death point out that "they had fulfilled all that was written of him" (Acts 13, 29). The appearances of the Risen One are the foundation of the apostolic testimony.

In the kerygma as such the above points formed merely an introduction to the witness itself and the call to repentance. In the circles of the Christian communities, however, they called for a further working out in the doctrine. This leads, after a certain time, to sketches of gospels being prepared — as Luke puts it: "Inasmuch as many have undertaken to compile a narrative of the things which have been accomplished among us. . . ." (Lk. 1, 1). These sketches and the entire preaching about Jesus' doings and teachings finally condensed into the four canonical gospels. The kernel from which they grew — or at any rate the oldest part — must have been the account of Jesus' suffering, death and

resurrection. This involves in its turn a close connection with memories of the Last Supper and with
the actual celebration of the Eucharist in the Christian community.

Intent of the Gospels

The gospels show that what Jesus did and taught
were the beginnings of a real revelation of his
identity as Messiah — which reaches its climax in
his death and resurrection. Mark portrays Jesus in
his earthly life as the one in whom God's reign is
coming — with power — to break Satan's rule. Jesus'
death and resurrection complete this victory.

They reveal the person of Jesus as the bearer and
source of salvation, as it breaks through completely
at his resurrection. A prime example of this is to
be found in John's gospel, where we are shown the
glory of the Son of God made man — "full of grace
and truth." Jesus indeed appears, here, as the Light,
the Life, the Bread-from-heaven, the Spring of
thirst-quenching water which is the Holy Spirit.

They clarify the nature of Jesus' mission and the
nature of the salvation with the aid of his words
and works. One could say that they give a com-
mentary about the Risen One's work of salvation,
based on the events of his earthly life. Jesus' own
statements explain better than any of the prophecies
the **meaning** of his death and resurrection. Then
there is the accentuation of the rescuing and universal

character of God's salvation — as shown e.g. by Jesus' special affection for the sinners in Luke.

They point out to the Church on earth the path for her own maintenance, from the words and deeds of Jesus. This is part of Matthew's main intention; he portrays Jesus as the Lawgiver for the new people of God.

It is sufficiently clear from the above that the four gospels as a whole are very closely connected with the kerygma. This is also shown by individual tendencies, such as Matthew's characteristic Kingdom-of-heaven theme, or the faith theme with John, where Old Testament texts are continually being applied to Jesus. Another interesting point is that the two gospels which differ most in form both **specifically** claim to be results of the kerygma. The title of Mark's gospel runs: "The beginning of the gospel of Jesus Christ, the Son of God"; the last part of John's gospel includes: "But these (miracles) are written that you may believe that Jesus is the Christ, the Son of God, and that believing you may have life in his name" (Jn. 20, 31). These words give the essence of the content and aims of the kerygma.

It can be stated that the kerygma became the inspiring and formative influence in the Christian community — above all through the gospels. It is in this way that Jesus himself became (and still is) the Teacher of his Church, just as he was that for his apostles.

The holy commandment

We can conclude from the apostolic letters and
from the gospels that the doctrine also occupied
itself intensively with the practice of Christian living.
There is no single writing in the New Testament
which gives a complete and ordered review of the
norms for Christian living. What we do find are
a number of fundamental commandments (e.g. in
the Sermon on the Mount). We find particularly the
call for love of God and our neighbor often repeated;
then there is a great variety of special norms and
regulations, most of them once again centered on
love of the neighbor; and finally we meet the
warnings against falling away from faith and against
pagan ways of life.

An extensive discussion of Christian morals would
be outside the scope of this chapter. We wish here
to give some attention to the connection between
the doctrine as dealing with Christian living and
the kerygma.

In the first place we note that acceptance of the
kerygma — in other words repentance and faith —
involves acceptance of a new way of life, a new
form of living. We find the confession of Jesus'
the Lord and Messiah, regularly described in the
Acts of the Apostles as "the Way" (cf. e.g. Acts 9, 2;
24, 14); this means that being a Christian is charac-
terized as a style of life based on belief in Jesus,
contrasting with other religious living-styles such as
the Jewish. In his letter to the Romans — urging
them to holiness of living — Paul typifies the Gospel

as a "standard of teaching" (Rom. 6, 17). He is
trying to put over the idea that teaching itself, which
accompanies the happy message of the kerygma, is
a kind of mold which shapes the life of the person
baptized. The New Testament often refers to the
way of life of Christians: "As therefore you received
Christ Jesus the Lord, so live in him" (Col. 2, 6).
This text shows clearly that being a Christian is a
form of living of which Christ — received in the
kerygma — is the definitive norm. Peter's second
letter equates "the knowledge of our Lord and
Savior Jesus Christ" with "the way of righteousness"
and the "holy commandment" (2 Pet. 2, 20-21). Paul
describes an ungodly and profligate life as being
"contrary to sound doctrine, in accordance with
the glorious gospel of the blessed God with which
I have been entrusted" (1 Tim. 1, 8-11).

The kerygma is therefore continued in a holy
commandment; via doctrine it gives a form to the
whole of life. But it is not only the general point
of departure for this teaching; it keeps returning,
in its various elements, in the numerous passages
of the apostolic letters which contain an exhortation
or specific instructions. It forms the motivation for
the exhortations; it is the background to the whole
of Christian living. We will further illuminate this
point with the aid of a number of texts.

First of all there is the theme of **calling** or election
to salvation. This has not yet been treated as such;
but it is contained in the concept of repentance and
faith as a gift of God (cf. p. 89); "for you know how,

like a father with his children, we exhorted each one of you and encouraged you and charged you to lead a life worthy of God, who calls you into his own kingdom and glory" (1 Thess. 2, 11-12). "As obedient children, do not be conformed to the passions of your former ignorance, but as he who called you is holy, be holy yourselves in all your conduct; since it is written: 'You shall be holy, for I am holy'" (1 Pet. 14-15). In both texts the exhortation to a holy life is accompanied by a pointing out of the election to faith and salvation. The first text contains furthermore the **Kingdom of God** theme. The second alludes — with the reference to the Old Testament — to the idea of the **people of God.** Belonging to the people of the holy God calls for holiness; and this means rejection of the typically pagan and unholy way of life, entry into the domain of the holy God, an attempt to recognize "what is the will of God, what is good and acceptable and perfect" (Rom. 12, 2; cf. also 2 Cor. 6, 14-7, 1).

The **Kingdom of God** theme also occurs in several texts which threaten unholy living with the penalty of exclusion from the kingdom: "Do not be deceived; neither the immoral, nor idolaters, nor adulterers, nor sensualists . . . will inherit the Kingdom of God. And such were some of you. But you were washed, you were sanctified, you were justified in the name of the Lord Jesus Christ and in the Spirit of our God" (1 Cor. 6, 9-11; cf. also Gal. 5, 19-21; Eph. 5, 5). We find a positive formulation of the same thought in Peter's first letter, derived from the salvation theme: "So put away all malice and all guile and insincerity and envy and all slander. Like newborn babes, long for the pure spiritual milk, that by it you grow up to salvation" (1 Pet. 2, 1-2). The pure spiritual milk is the pure doctrine, the food for a way of living which leads to salvation.

In innumerable texts dealing with Christian living we meet the kerygmatic theme of Christ as **the risen Lord and the new nature** (i.e. of mankind). "Cleanse out the old leaven that you may be a new dough, as you really are unleavened. For Christ, our paschal Lamb, has been sacrified" (1 Cor. 5, 7). "The body is not meant for immorality, but for the Lord, and the Lord for the body. And God raised the Lord and will also raise us up by his power" (1 Cor. 6, 13-14). "If then you have been raised with Christ, seek the things that are above, where Christ is, seated at the right hand of God. Set your minds on things that are above, not on things that are on earth. For you have died, and your life is hid with Christ in God. When Christ who is our life appears, then you also will appear with him in glory. Put to death therefore what is earthly in you: immorality, impurity, passion, evil desire, and covetousness. . . . Do not lie to one another, seeing that you have put off the old nature with its practices and have put on the new nature, which is being renewed in knowledge after the image of its Creator" (Col. 3, 1-9). In these and in many other texts, Christian living is seen as a contrast to badness and impurity. The intrinsic ground for this is the unity with the glorified Lord, the wearing of the new nature. It is a requirement which is not merely externally

made of the baptized individual, it is a **fait accompli**
which forces itself upon him. Since however this
established situation also has the form of a command,
Paul can say elsewhere that the Christian **must** put
on the Lord, clothe himself with the new nature
(cf. Rom. 13, 14; Eph. 4, 20-24). Having been raised
up with the Lord, the baptized individual is light
in the Lord — and must live as a child of the light
(Eph. 5, 8-9; cf. also 1 Thess. 5, 4-11). This is an
inner necessity for him.

The text of Col. 3, 1-9 which we mentioned a
moment ago also opens a vista on **the Day of Christ,**
the coming (verse 4). See for this also Phil. 1, 9-11:
"And it is my prayer that your love may abound
more and more, with knowledge and all discern-
ment, so that you may approve what is excellent,
and may be pure and blameless for the Day of
Christ, filled with the fruits of righteousness which
come through Jesus Christ, to the glory and praise
of God." In the same way that Christian living is a
growing toward salvation (1 Pet. 2, 2), it is also a
growing toward the day of Christ. This must be a
stimulus to rich fruit of righteousness, to perfection
(cf. also Phil. 3, 12-16; 2 Pet. 3, 10-14).

The earliest **paraenetic** (i.e. dealing with "the
'coming") passage in Paul's letters mentions —
besides the theme of calling by the Father and the
Lord's day of judgment — also the **gift of the Holy
Spirit.** After an exhortation to holiness and a warning against misbehavior, Paul continues: "Because
the Lord (Christ) is the avenger in all these things

(the sinful practices), as we solemnly forewarned you.
For God has not called us for uncleanness, but in
holiness. Therefore whoever disregards this, disregards not man but God, who gives his Holy Spirit
to you" (1 Thess. 4, 3-8; cf. also the above-quoted
text of 1 Cor. 6, 9-11, and 1 Cor. 6, 19). Just like the
union with Christ, the gift of the Spirit — which
means sanctification, devotion to the holy God —
necessarily calls for a penetration of this sanctification into every aspect of the way of life. This means
a dedication of one's life to God (cf. also Rom. 12, 1).

The above-quoted texts — which are a selection
from many — make it sufficiently clear that the
doctrine regarding the holy commandment, regarding
holy Christian living, is backed up by the kerygma.
From this it follows that Christian living seen in a
negative sense — as rejection of badness and impurity — or in the positive sense of goodness, love
of neighbor, service to God — is to be treated as a
postulate, in itself a necessary consequence of being
a Christian. This is its real reason of existence,
from this standpoint it can be compellingly motivated.
Christian living is **the full penetration of the kerygma
into all action,** nothing else. This standpoint is com-
pactly formulated in the letter of James: "Therefore
put away all filthiness and rank growth of wicked-
ness and receive with meekness the implanted word,
which is able to save your souls" (Jas. 1, 21). The
germinal force of the kerygma's word — accepted in
a spirit of learning — results in the putting aside of
all impurity and badness, leading us thereby to our
definitive salvation.

10

THE PREACHING AS AN ACT
OF SALVATION BY GOD

As a message of salvation — confronting mankind with a supernatural reality — the preaching is in fact a coming of God into this world. It is not merely a presentation of salvation, an announcement of God's plan with the requirements to be met by mankind, but it is an **act of salvation by God.** It is his first act of salvation. Jesus' mission began with the message about the Kingdom of God; and after his resurrection, as salvation coursed over the world, we find always that the first impetus is given by the apostolic kerygma.

The Old Testament considered the prophetic word to be charged with godly power. It seems only to be expected that the New Testament does not treat the preaching merely as an external interpretation of salvation: in fact, the preaching is seen as that aspect of the reality of salvation itself by which this makes its entry into the world.

The nature of the preaching as an act of salvation by God can be approached from various directions.

Word and work

The preaching by Jesus and the apostles is accompanied by **miracles,** also referred to as "works" of God. In the gospels and in the Acts we find that miracles are a regularly recurring element, while the apostolic letters also mention them. The miracles in themselves are a sign of the messianic age — a visible and tangible realization of salvation — as foretold by the prophets. Jesus points this out to John the Baptist, when the latter sends a messenger to him with this question: "Are you he who is to come, or shall we look for another?" Jesus answers: "Go and tell John what you hear and see: the blind receive sight and the lame walk, lepers are cleansed and the deaf hear, and the dead are raised up, and the poor have the good news (gospel) preached to them" (Mt. 11, 2-5). These words contain an implied but nontheless clear reference to Old Testament prophecy (cf. Is. 26, 19; 35, 5-6; 61, 1). Jesus' answer means this: the miracles which he performs are a fulfillment of the prophecies — and therefore a first realization of the messianic salvation. The miracles are — according to a frequently used term — "mighty deeds" by the God of salvation.

At the same time, however, we find that the miracles are directly associated with the preaching. This is already present in the text of Mt. 11, 5 above. They attract public attention to the preacher who performs them, or whose appearance they accompany; he is God's ambassador and they form the divine seal of his preaching. In this sense they are referred to as signs. It is particularly in John's gospel that this "sign" character of the miracles is made clear. Jesus says to the Jews: ". . . for the works which the Father has granted me to accomplish, these very works which I am doing, bear me witness that the Father has sent me" (Jn. 5, 36). The works too, the miracles themselves, have a language of their own — in which they bear witness to Christ. ". . . even though you do not believe me," says Jesus, "believe the works" (Jn. 10, 38). Peter describes Jesus to the people of Jerusalem as "a man attested to you by God with mighty work and wonders and signs which God did through him in your midst, as you yourselves know" (Acts 2, 22). Regarding the apostles it is said. "They went forth and preached everywhere, while the Lord worked with them and confirmed the message by the signs that attended it" (Mk. 16, 20). While Paul and Barnabas preached, the Lord "bore witness to the word of his grace, granting signs and wonders to be done by their hands" (Acts 14, 3; cf. also Hebr. 2, 4). "Signs and wonders and mighty works" are the "signs of a true apostle" (2 Cor. 12, 12).

Preaching and miracles, words and works really amount to one great revelation of God's power — with the preaching as starting point. Numerous texts assume this unity of word and work. After Jesus' death it was declared that he "was a prophet mighty in deed and word before God and all the people" (Lk. 24, 19; cf. also Rom. 15, 18-19). This unity on its own is already sufficient grounds for

the statement that the preaching is a revelation of
God's power, the beginnings of his salvation in this
world.

The word, charged with power

The preaching as such, however, is also charged
with divine power; it is in itself an act of God's
might, no less than the miracle. We may perhaps
already read this thought in a few texts which do
not differentiate between word and work, but which
treat the entire apostolic activity as a series of great
deeds by God. Paul and Barnabas reported in
Jerusalem to "the apostles and elders . . . all that
God had done with them" (Acts 15, 4; the context
is that of the first missionary journey and the conversion of the pagans; cf. also Acts 14, 27; 21, 19).

In the Old Testament the prophetic word was
thought of as a dynamic and creative reality. The
New Testament, it is clear, applies the same thought
to the preaching. First of all the preaching itself
is seen as a **messianic occurrence.** After Jesus has
read out in the Nazareth synagogue the Isaiah text
about the good news of redemption and grace for
God's people, he goes on to say: "Today this scripture has been fulfilled **in your hearing**" (Lk. 4, 16-21).
There can be only one meaning for this; through
Jesus' **words,** which he now speaks the ancient
prophecy is fulfilled and the messianic salvation
becomes reality. The same thing is implied in the
text of Mt. 11, 5; besides the actual miracles we
find the preaching of the gospel to the poor given
as a sign of the messianic age.

What is valid for Jesus' preaching may also be applied to the preaching by the apostles. Many texts state or imply, indeed, that their preaching is **carried by God's power,** which is operative in what they say. There is power behind the preaching: "With great power the apostles gave their testimony to the resurrection of the Lord Jesus" (Acts 4, 33). "My speech and my message were not in plausible words of wisdom, but in demonstration of the Spirit and power, that your faith might not rest in the wisdom of men but in the power of God (1 Cor. 2, 4-5). The preaching itself is a "power of God" (1 Cor. 1, 18). The power which enlivens the apostles' preaching is the power of the Holy Spirit, which Jesus had promised (cf. Acts 1, 8; Jn. 15, 26-27). The glorified Christ is speaking through the preacher, since he lives in him and in the community of the faithful, with the power of his resurrection: "You desire proof that Christ is speaking in me. He is not weak in dealing with you, but is powerful in you. For he was crucified in weakness, but lives by the power of God. For we are weak in him, but in dealing with you we shall live with him by the power of God" (2 Cor. 13, 3-4).

Just like the prophetic word in the Old Testament, the preaching of the word in the New Testament is personified. It is then described as a something which is **charged with power** and which spreads and works through that power: "So the word of the Lord grew and prevailed mightily" (Acts 19, 20; cf. also p. 3). These and similar texts are not to be interpreted as mere figures of speech; they are backed up by the dynamic aspect of the prophetic word, which shall accomplish that which God intends (Is. 55, 10-11).

The New Testament concept of the creative power of the word is most pointedly formulated in the following texts. They attribute the redemption and the rebirth to the preaching of the word. "Of his own will he brought us forth by the word of truth that we should be a kind of first fruits of his creatures" (Jas. 1, 18). "Receive with meekness the implanted word, which is able to save your souls" (Jas. 1, 21). "You have been born anew, not of perishable seed but of imperishable, through the living and abiding word of God. . . . This word is the good news which was preached to you" (1 Pet. 1, 23-25). These texts present the word, the preached word, as a lifegerm full of God's creative power — as the seed of the rebirth, the instrument of God's will of salvation.

Statements like these also throw light on other texts, enabling us to understand them in their full import. When Paul, for example, describes the Gospel as "the power of God for salvation to every one who has faith" (Rom. 1, 16), or says that Jesus Christ "brought life and immortality to light through the Gospel" (2 Tim. 1, 10), then he is seeing the preaching of the gospel undoubtedly as the power-charged instrument of God's salvation. This instrument is like a two-sided sword however (cf. Hebr. 4, 12), which brings the unbelievers to judgment: "He who rejects me and does not receive my sayings has a judge; the word that I have spoken will be his judge on the last day" (Jn. 12, 48).

We see therefore that the preaching is an act of salvation by God, because his redemptive power works through it. The outward visibility of this power is in the accompanying miracle or sign; internally the power can be appreciated through the word's characteristic but mysterious effectiveness. Theologically this working of the preached word requires a further clarification — particularly in connection with the effectiveness of the sacramental word — but the working itself cannot be denied, if we bear the Scriptures in mind. It would be furthermore an unjustified narrowing of the biblical thought, if we were only to consider Christ's and the apostles' preaching as a real act of salvation. We must include the Church's preaching through all the centuries, at least so long as we consider the Church to be the heir of the apostolic mission.

Word and Church-community

This last conclusion has its importance for the relation between the function of the preaching and the Church-community. Since apostolic times the Church-community has existed and has been growing mainly through the preaching of the word. The New Testament frequently refers to the faithful as "the called ones," referring to their real participation in salvation; and Paul writes to the faithful of Thessalonica that God has called them **through his Gospel** (2 Thess. 2, 13-14). This admittedly is the only place where a specific causal connection is given between preaching and calling, but the connection is implied throughout the above-quoted texts. God calls to salvation, not only through the inner urging by the Spirit, but also by the power of the herald's word of the preaching (the kerygma). Furthermore, the people are called to salvation "in the one body" (Col. 3, 15) — in the community of the Church. This enables us to conclude that God's act of salvation in the preaching, his loud proclamation of this salvation, has **called the community of the faithful together and is still calling them together.**

The New Testament shows us how the preaching is completed and terminated in baptism, the laying-on of hands and the breaking of bread — i.e. the celebration of the Eucharist (cf. Acts 2, 40-42; 8, 14-17). The preaching therefore also has a **cult-**import. It is the herald's calling together of God's people for "the solemn assembly" (cf. Joel 1, 14; 2, 15), at which they approach the Father — in sacrifice and sacrament — through Christ, who sanctifies them and fills them with his Spirit.

The preaching of the word continues its operation in this sanctified community. Paul writes that the "word of God . . . is at work in you believers" (1 Thess. 2, 13; cf. also 2 Thess. 3, 1). It is the manifestation of the Spirit in the community (cf. 1 Cor. 12, 7-11; Hebr. 2, 4), as words of wisdom, admonition and compassion (as in 1 Cor. 1, 4-6; 1 Pet. 4, 11) in praise of God: "Let the word of Christ dwell in you richly, as you teach and admonish one another in all wisdom, and as you sing psalms and hymns and spiritual songs with thankfulness in your hearts to God" (Col. 3, 16).

In this way may the community of God's people — reborn and sustained by the living word of the preaching — "taste the kindness of the Lord" and grow up by the power of this word to everlasting salvation (cf. 1 Pet. 1, 23; 2-3).

The preaching of the word among us is a lasting realization of salvation. Nowhere does God's salvation come to us in such a human form as in the preaching. This can however become a stumbling-block for us, in two ways. In the first place we can forget the divine power of the word because of the human — sometimes, alas, too human — wrapping in which it is presented. Alternatively we can forget the Cross — which is at the heart of God's word — and desire to preach, or hear preaching, in words of purely human wisdom. We can avoid this two-fold trap through a living contact with God's word in holy Scripture, which is derived from preaching and bears witness to this preaching. This was after all the way in which God's salvation came into the world for all time.